Oral History in Your Library

ORAL HISTORY IN YOUR LIBRARY

Create Shelf Space for Community Voice

Cyns Nelson

with contributions by Adam Speirs

Foreword by **R. David Lankes**

LIBRARIES UNLIMITED™

An Imprint of ABC-CLIO, LLC

Santa Barbara, California • Denver, Colorado

Library of Congress Cataloging-in-Publication Data

Names: Nelson, Cyns, author. | Speirs, Kristofer Adam, author. | Lankes, R. David, 1970- writer of foreword.
Title: Oral history in your library : create shelf space for community voice / Cyns Nelson ; with contributions by Adam Speirs ; foreword by R. David Lankes.
Description: Santa Barbara, California : Libraries Unlimited, an imprint of ABC-CLIO, LLC, [2018] | Includes bibliographical references and index.
Identifiers: LCCN 2018010718 (print) | LCCN 2018024695 (ebook) | ISBN 9781440857256 (ebook) | ISBN 9781440857249 (paperback: alk. paper)
Subjects: LCSH: Libraries—Special collections—Oral history. | Libraries—Special collections—History, Local. | Oral history. | Libraries and community.
Classification: LCC Z688.O52 (ebook) | LCC Z688.O52 N45 2018 (print) | DDC 025.2/79—dc23
LC record available at https://lccn.loc.gov/2018010718

ISBN: 978–1–4408–5724–9 (paperback)
       978–1–4408–5725–6 (ebook)

22 21 20 19 18   1 2 3 4 5

This book is also available as an eBook.

Libraries Unlimited
An Imprint of ABC-CLIO, LLC

ABC-CLIO, LLC
130 Cremona Drive, P.O. Box 1911
Santa Barbara, California 93116-1911
www.abc-clio.com

This book is printed on acid-free paper ∞

Manufactured in the United States of America

Illustrations created for this title by Bobby Small, Doodler. Used with permission.

Contents

Foreword

I was presenting at a pop-up library in Tilburg. The town in the Netherlands was an historic center for building and maintaining trains. In recent times, the train industry had moved overseas. The town was in the process of reclaiming warehouses and huge open workshops once used to build and repair engines and railcars. The new space was opened up to entrepreneurs and start-ups. One of the massive open floors would house the new library. The pop-up library was an experimental space for librarians and the community to come together and play with new configurations and services for the library once it moved.

This is not an unusual story. Across the world, spaces meant for large industries are being converted into spaces for a new economy. What was different was that the library set up a large interactive kiosk in the middle of the experimental space. Community members could use the kiosk to learn about the train industry and the history of the space. Once again, not particularly innovative. That is until I found out that the kiosk was the result of an oral history project. The kiosk was accessing the memories, the memorabilia, and the stories of train workers.

You could click on a floor plan, a picture, or an artifact and hear the reality of these things through the world of those who built the space and those who worked in it. Visiting workers were invited to add their own memories and stories. For me, it was an amazing example of seeing a community as a true collection of a library. It was the power of oral history.

In the book in your hands, Cyns Nelson shows in the most wonderful way the reality that knowledge is uniquely human and created through conversations (including with ourselves). If libraries are in the knowledge business, they are in the conversation business. They are in the creation business. They are in the business of helping people make meaning in their lives.

The oral history methods detailed in these pages make these sentiments practical and present.

Our communities are brilliant. The experiences of plumbers and doctors, of layers and stay-at-home parents, professors and writers and illustrators and teachers and barbers and clerks and children form the rich tapestry woven together by the interactions of communities. Using oral history techniques, this community fabric can be instrumental in advancing the aspirations of the community.

This book, these techniques, the very idea of using oral histories within a community are more than nice pieces of outreach. They are a real statement that the stories of a community—the results of members making meaning of their lives—are valuable, and therefore, so are the communities themselves. Too often librarians and the libraries they build and maintain focus on the problems and deficits of people. A library seeks to improve literacy, to help the unemployed, or to enrich the lives of children. In other words, librarians feel the community is illiterate, unemployed, and isolated. An oral history project says, "your lives and your stories are the most valuable asset we have as a community, and as a library, we are going to help share that with the world."

I know you will find Cyns Nelson's work here approachable and pragmatic. What I hope you also see is that she is providing a blueprint for centering the librarian in the community, and the community in the library. Don't be fooled by the prose and reassurance in the book—while she is talking about oral histories from her vast experience, she is also inviting you to think differently about your community and your library. I love it.

R. David Lankes

Preface

In 2005, as an adult student of library science, I attended a daylong conference of the Society of Rocky Mountain Archivists. I was there because one of the members had offered to pay the registration cost, and at the time, my interests were broad and unsettled—so I jumped at the offer. For that particular meeting, a theme was oral history—something I'd never considered. Many of the participants described challenges or outright barriers faced when dealing with oral history as a "material." A good portion of the obstructions, by my observation, were mental hurdles, owing to the unusualness of interviews compared to more static documents associated with archival collections.

Then came Wendy Hall, branch manager from Boulder's Carnegie Library for Local History, home to the Maria Rogers Oral History Program (MROHP). Boulder pursued interviews and had established a thriving program that normalized the treatment of oral history. By the date of the conference, close to 1,500 interviews had been digitized (or were born digital) and were being placed online for listening. This accomplishment seemed exceptional, and my imagination was captivated. I was drawn, first, to the idea of recorded interviews as a primary information source. And then, seeing that a public library could instigate the creation, collection, and dissemination of oral histories ... well, brilliant! (I thought.)

Two years later, I became a volunteer intern, learning about the Maria Rogers program and their process for integrating oral histories into the library's collection and mission. Also, I learned how extraordinary was the prototype—in terms of setting, approach, scale, and product. A rare model. And when the position for oral history coordinator opened, again I jumped.

Flash forward to May 2016 and the Public Library Association's annual meeting at the Convention Center in Denver, Colorado. I never had participated in events of the PLA—while I had presented to the American Library Association and regularly attended meetings of the Oral History Association,

Society of American Archivists, and regional library/archives gatherings. Adam
Speirs asked if I would join a panel that focused on oral history in public-
library settings, and without hesitation I agreed. I was eager to share a picture
of our work at the Carnegie Library and our function in the Boulder Public
Library system. I knew that my job—entirely dedicated to oral history—was
unique if not singular in a public-library setting. Our panel had a large audience
and ran out of time to respond to all of the questions and comments. Success!

Shortly after the PLA conference, I received an email from an acquisitions
editor at Libraries Unlimited. She referenced the conference and asked if
I would be interested in writing a book on the subject of oral history and
libraries. A desire for expertise seemed evident from the attendance and
quantity of questions raised during the PLA session. My informal observa-
tions over the years also pointed to this gap in attention to the subject.
Nonetheless, I had not considered the idea, and I said as much: I did not
see a book inside of me—a thick pamphlet, maybe.

Putting this manuscript together, I've been able to reflect on the stepping
stones that have emerged to support my passions and my forward progress.
Also, I've noticed a similar phenomenon for oral history and the library that
I now call home. Was Boulder simply lucky to have a "Maria Rogers" in the
community? She was the first to ensure that personal experiences were made
part of the library experience; she was the catalyst for organizing an oral history program; most important, she invited others to participate in her oral
history movement.[1]

At the same time, Boulder Public Library must be credited for recognizing
the importance of what Maria started, for supporting her vision and helping
ensconce oral history as a valued component of the library's mission.
MROHP was born out of a collective recognition for oral history's power;
let this recognition find its way to you and your library.

NOTE

1. If you want to view an inspired take on the idea leadership, try Derek Sivers's
YouTube video, "How to Start a Movement"—alternately referred to as "First
Follower: Leadership Lessons from a Dancing Guy."

Introduction

Library Science, Not Rocket Science

INSPIRATION

Even before turning the pages of R. David Lankes's *Atlas of New Librarianship*, I anticipated a resource of critical insight that would charge my sentiments and energies. I was not disappointed. Navigating Lankes's *Atlas*, I filled notebook pages with quotes and revelations that walked hand-in-hand with the inspiration and purpose for this book. Lankes structures his *Atlas* according to threads that stem from his mission statement for librarians: *The Mission of Librarians Is to Improve Society through Facilitating Knowledge Creation in Their Communities*. In turn, statements from Lankes's *Atlas* are warp and woof to the mission/purpose of this text. Here, you will not be getting a "How to" book but a "Why to" and "Can do" invocation.

In the scope of his *Atlas*, Lankes calls for a "reexamination of functions and assumptions." My call is similarly poised to challenge behaviors that have governed librarians' relationship to oral history.

- I believe in the power of information to improve the human condition.
- I believe that firsthand accounts present the most impacting kind of information.
- I believe that oral history—the key vehicle for obtaining firsthand accounts—must be made prevalent and pertinent to our frameworks for sharing information.
- Finally, I believe that public libraries *are* the framework for delivering on the promise inherent in oral history's potential.

EXPLANATION/NAVIGATION

Purpose

Many fine books have been written for the purpose of instructing oral history technique, methodology, and practice. Also, books emphasizing curatorial principles as well as cataloging instructions are available. This book invites librarians, specifically, to bring their skills and training into oral history field work. The intent is to alter perceptions about oral history's place in library settings, particularly public libraries. The goal is to remove any hesitance for working with oral history and, instead, move library and information professionals to embrace the potential and possibility, envisioning the path forward. Librarians should become instigators of oral history, not passive recipients of audio files.

Scope

The organization of this book is simple. Main chapters address the question of how individual story gets transformed into shared knowledge, based on four Rs: **Recognize, Record, Represent,** and **Reach.** *Recognize* the unique value of oral history, *record* the stories, *represent* the content, and *reach* an audience. Each R is correlated with a specific tenet of library/information science: Recognize = Collection Development, Record = Preservation, Represent = Organization, and Reach = Dissemination. You will find one chapter for each R, and the ideas build on one another—sequential reading helps ensure that the whole picture makes sense. Chapter Five expands on concepts pulled from David Lankes's *Atlas,* showing how the threads of "new librarianship" are at home with the suggestions in this book, and Chapter Six demonstrates the positive returns of making oral history part of your library, using the example of the Maria Rogers Oral History Program at Boulder Public Library.

In seven different places, you will find succinct dives into topics that may add practical or technical detail—ideas that warrant further consideration but could distract from the narrative flow and big-picture presentation. These contributions, by Adam Speirs, were written in response/reaction to his reading of main chapters.

Audience and Use

Considering each of the sections and subsections—and in determining the focus of discussion—two guiding principles were held: **Librarian Lens** and **Durable Content.** Librarian lens: What do *librarians* need to know? What will connect with librarian thinking? You might be in admin, collection development, programming, or special services; or maybe you wear a variety of hats and are working in a small, independent library. If you are someone who wants a relationship with your community, this book offers a means to that end. Durable content: Acknowledging the limits of any book, the highest aim for this title is a presentation of ideas that can be exercised over time, regardless of how tools and technologies change. In this book, you will not be pushed toward a specific brand of equipment or prescribed a particular software; in this book, you will be guided toward channels of thinking that can help you navigate the questions of today, tomorrow, and the days after.

Recognize = Collection Development

Tell me about your collection development policy: What is the purpose and the reasoning? What guides your decisions? Traditional understanding of collection development includes material acquisition, replacement, and weeding, along with planning for new collection areas in accordance with library mission and resources. These same principles are applied to the engagement of oral history to help facilitate knowledge creation in your community. Chapter One describes your process for becoming aware of oral history's possibilities and its power. This chapter is about your own revelation—understanding the power you hold for being an agent of knowledge creation. Unlike material acquisitions that must be selected from an existing body of logged titles, the development of oral history comes from a place of imagination for what *can* exist.

With oral history, you are pulling together primary sources that become part of your library's identity (a.k.a., developing a collection). At the same time, you are gathering multiple perspectives that represent different viewpoints (a.k.a., "collective" development). The goal is to establish the breadth of truths that exist around a specific topic, event, or life experience. Data points such as names, locations, and time periods can help build facts, while oral history builds truths—in the sense that ten individuals all can be present for an event that is factually pinpointed, and each of those ten might describe a unique experience. Think about the story of the blind men and the elephant: all are touching the same animal but in different parts, and all come to separate conclusions about what the animal is like.[1] For an observer to receive a complete picture of the elephant—metaphorically speaking— he or she must be exposed to the full array of accounts. All of the puzzle pieces must be identified, placed in proximity to one another, and exposed. The presentation of a full picture is the goal for oral history, and it is the goal for the library in pursuing interview sets.

VISION

reality is
imagination that has
become consensus

The vision for this book is a new reality where oral history is a thriving, vibrant information source that libraries use to facilitate knowledge creation in their communities. A starting point for this picture is the Progression Model, which describes precedents of behavior toward oral history and behavioral shifts that catalyze new opportunities. The "precedents"—worn paths of convention—largely are patterns observed in the United States, while shifts can be taking hold anywhere. (The International Oral History Association has a growing body of practitioners, and countries other than the United States—Australia, the United Kingdom, and Canada—are attentive to oral history's potential.)

Oral History: Explanation of Centrality

To buy the picture I'm selling, a reader first must agree that oral history merits focused consideration. Oral history is the intentional recollection,

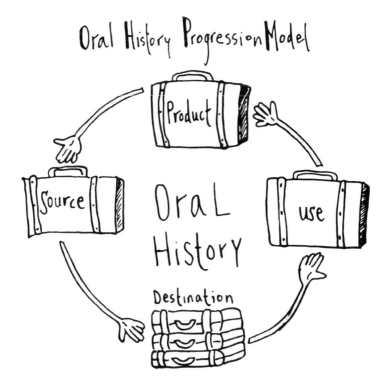

capture, and preservation of memories. It is a tool for creating firsthand information, and it also is a primary source that embodies individual knowledge that has been seasoned over time.[2] Information is the most potent change agent; oral history is uniquely informative and can move people from awareness to understanding and to empathy. Firsthand stories challenge traditional and filtered types of documentation; stories authenticate our picture of the human experience and our mindset for understanding human actions and aspirations. For these reasons, I am asking you—for the duration of this book—to make oral history the center of your focus and to accept the centrality of its importance.

Also, before going forward, I must note the conditions providing context for this book's objective:

a) awareness for *story* as a structure for sensemaking;

b) blurred lines between oral history, storytelling, and recorded dialogue/conversation;

c) the ubiquity of digital recording devices and thus the explosion of opportunities for creating audio and/or video; and

d) a predicament in which libraries feel overwhelmed by the uncustomary and complicated package of oral history.

Source: Where Does Oral History Come From?

Precedent: Historically, oral history has been a practice of specific disciplines for narrow purposes defined by individual practitioners such as researchers, historians, and folklorists. Oral history was a means to an end, maybe a thesis or book. Individuals who engaged in oral history likely would have been allied with a university.[3]

Shift: Oral history can be a practice of communities—social, religious, organizational, and neighborly—for varied but specified reasons defined by need and opportunity. The interview becomes a conscious act of creation with the recording itself as an end. (Note: I'm purposefully not saying *the* end, rather *an* end.) The oral history then germinates from agencies of community, such as neighborhood organizations, faith affiliations, or the local library. *Library* must be considered an agency of community.

Destination: Where Does Oral History Go? How Is It Dealt With?

Precedent: With few exceptions, such as the Library of Congress, major oral history projects and repositories in the United States are associated with universities. If an oral history has come from a researcher, and if the researcher is of a mind to donate the interview (interviews plural, more likely), the donation setting often is an institutional archive. Picture the not-so-proverbial shoebox that gets handed to a fastidious curator. Archives can be marvelous stewards of cultural heritage and documentation. Also, with a focus on preservation, the archives might be a safe landing spot for the medium that carries the oral history interview (e.g., reel-to-reel, cassette, paper transcript). The question of how the content is dealt with becomes less crisp.

The archival process for organizing and describing materials relies on context being supplied from somewhere.[4] Archives customarily deal with voluminous donated collections, and the principles for organizing such collections rarely allow item-level attention. In addition, archives with an emphasis on preservation have not been proactive in making holdings accessible. Oral history, especially, has been marginalized as a difficult "object" to manage and share.[5]

Shift: Libraries can diversify their holdings by including oral history interviews. In choosing to work with oral history, the library demonstrates that community voice matters. Oral history cultivates a nonproprietary and sustainable resource in personal experience; it invites promotional, programming, collaborative, and creative opportunities. Oral history shows the library to be a place of connection and participation. Circulation of materials is central to the library mindset, and libraries have protocols for establishing maximum accessibility for materials. An oral history can be treated like a book, a movie, or any other item for checkout. Being *checked out* (a.k.a., heard) is the objective for all recorded narratives.

Use: How Is Oral History Made Useful? How Is It Used?

Precedent: The first modern U.S. oral history program, the Columbia Oral History Research Office, created transcripts from taped interviews and then gave no further consideration to the original recording—going so far as to reuse the cassette and record over existing interviews. The practical justification pointed to researchers' preference for the transcript, and only "folklorists, linguists, and ethnomusicologists wanted to hear the sound recordings" (Ritchie 2003, 67). By the 1970s, archives offered a transcript, index/summary, and audio (or video) as records of the oral history. Opinions have evolved, opportunities have expanded, and I doubt that any archive would willfully destroy a sound recording, even if the quality was exceptionally poor. On the contrary, recent academic discussion extols the "orality" of oral history, and major institutions with interview collections have been devising tools for pushing researchers to listen.[6] Still, further progress is needed; the conversation should not lean narrowly on academics, archives, and researchers.

Shift: Oral history will achieve its potential when firsthand knowledge is made *prevalent* and *pertinent* to our public frameworks for understanding and sharing information. Prevalent = widely accepted, practiced, or favored. Pertinent = clearly relevant. The challenge, then, is to create these conditions for oral history—and doing so, to expand/redefine who is using interviews and for what applications. Libraries are appreciated by the public, they are trusted, and they are utilized. Placing oral history in libraries and having interviews mixed with other types of expected information (books, magazines, journals, etc.) would demonstrate the equal value of individual experience. Personal stories would be positioned for wide distribution, and people would think of oral history as a go-to source of information due to its availability. Just as important, interviews must show themselves to be germane to public interest, inquiry, and thirst for understanding. The surrogate information (metadata) that populates a catalog or other retrieval system needs to be meaningful and well-constructed. Community must see the direct relevance of engaging with oral history.

Product: What Is Created from Oral History?

The practice of oral history brings outcomes both tangible and intangible. **Precedent:** Oral history consistently has been a means for creating new documentation, new awareness, and new understanding. Primarily, the recipient of these "news" has been the individual researcher—either the person conducting the interview for independent reasons or the researcher who seeks primary sources as data points for an independent project, such as a book. The outcome is both a new artifact (i.e., book) and market space for the ideas and expressions contained within the book.

Shift: By making oral history a communal practice and one supported systemically by libraries, more awareness is created, along with more understanding and more types of new documentation. The shift is one of scale: more product and more production value.

IDENTIFYING NEED AND OPPORTUNITY

The occasion for establishing an oral history collection arises from need or opportunity: Something motivates the action. The impetus may be internal to the library—such as a desire to diversify the content being offered—or it may come from the community—such as an event that galvanizes public attention. Either way, the job is to be attentive to what is happening in relation to your library and community. What events are taking place? What *has* taken place? What conversations are you hearing and observing? Are people getting what they need from the library? What does the library need—and how might oral history assist with a delivered outcome?

Good for the Library: Don't be reluctant to claim oral history for its advantageous prospects. Maybe you have a board that includes influential members of the community and, even, connections to deep pockets. Does a library exist that could not make excellent use of more financial resources? Be vocal about your intent to capture the experiences of your community and be clear about the benefit. Make oral history the feather in your cap. Talk about how your library will steward one-of-a-kind information sets and will mirror the activities of the community. Take suggestions for subject areas to explore, and take kudos (and contributions) for doing the work.

Good for the Community: Collection development is about filling the gap between what people know and what they need to know; where they are at and where they could be. The art of the reference interview is instructive to the development of an oral history collection. When trying to determine what source will help an individual (and where it can be found), you may discover that your library can be the creator of the source. And the process of involving your community—literally using their voices—will empower all participants.

COLLECT THEIR ENERGY

It is difficult to run a successful oral history program yourself and have time for anything else, including patrons. So, reliance on volunteers is a must, whether they are students completing assigned interviews or local history buffs making good use of their time. How can these folks contribute best to the overall value of your library's oral history program and collections? The care and interest they show is directly tied to the value of what they produce.

Two widely successful programs, the Civil Rights and Veterans History Projects out of the American Folklife Center at the Library of Congress, are so successful because the people participating in them are invested to begin with. The volunteer interviewers already WANT to make a difference and already have an interest in the subject matter. Library of Congress supplies some basic training pamphlets and an instructional website, and volunteers from all over the United States have contributed 75,000+ interviews to their collections. They are model programs.

The Civil Rights Movement and World War II are defining moments in American history. Your community also has booms or busts. Long-standing traditions define places, as do long-standing institutions. People in your community are invested in those moments and historical arcs, and they need a channel for their energy. Supply that channel through the archetypal library activity: instruction.

Volunteers will have questions about how to start, what questions to ask, whom to ask questions, where they should ask questions, and so on. At every step in the process, supply the resources they need to do what they set out to do. It will be time consuming, so make that up-front investment of time pay off by documenting every question resolved. And as you build out, ask the most advanced volunteers to use that documentation to become trainers themselves. They will demonstrate enthusiasm for the work to new volunteers and will model the effort required to build solid collections.

Tools and empowerment yield great returns, but make sure to establish boundaries early on. The librarian's expertise rightly lies in the library: in library systems, theory, and practice. Empowering volunteers to be the subject matter experts of your collections and build relationships with the community around the subject strengthens the collections' value; it frees the librarian to focus on librarianship. When volunteers have the training and autonomy, they will mostly take care of themselves, and you.

At Douglas County Libraries, we had digital recorders available for checkout through the local history department, and we would provide copies of interview forms to interviewers. Fairly regularly, we would get a call from a volunteer who would effectively say, "I have an interview scheduled for Sunday. Can I have a recorder ready to pick up on Friday?" On Monday, he would bring back the recorder and paperwork, along with any donated supplementary materials (photos,

letters) and be on his merry way. He had deep connections in the community, knew his domain, and would line up interviews himself—no
problem. His biggest need from the library, perhaps his only need if
you consider the forms and equipment convenience, was for us to take
what was created and make it publicly accessible.

Adam Spiers

USING ORAL SOURCES TO COMPLEMENT
OR ILLUMINATE HOLDINGS

As with any investment, the decision to pursue oral history should be strategic, looking for a return or reward. Two types of oral history exist: Life and
Topic. With Life interviews, the narrator himself or herself is the subject of
inquiry; the objective is to document that individual's life experiences through
one or more interviews. Individuals would be selected for contributions to the
community, activities, and accomplishments. A person need not be famous to
be interviewed—in fact, notoriety might be a reason to place an individual at
low priority. If the person's life already is fully explored through existing documentation, the information gleaned during an oral history might be duplicative.
In particular, individuals who are high profile might have a canned set of
responses to life questions—and do you need to have the same stories repeated
for your library collection? Or does another set of stories exist, which might
counter the predominant narrative? Who are the people to tell *those* stories?

Topical interviews are focused on a subject or event, which then is
explored through multiple narrators who have specific knowledge or experience related to the subject. The chosen topic should be something that is
definitively relevant to the community and might be in peril of going undocu-
mented (e.g., the people who are informed on the topic are at risk of not
being able to share their experiences). Maybe your city has a large population of immigrants who have spent years in the community, participating in
the social fabric, and whose status recently has become imperiled. Or maybe
you have an organization of volunteer firefighters or rescuers who never have
been asked to share the stories of their work. A concerted plan is key to this
type of project. Once the topic has been decided, *perspectives* must be identified and then individuals named who can speak from those perspectives.
Time periods also might be part of the equation, if the topic spans decades.
A planning grid helps organize a project. Mary Larson, at Oklahoma State
University, assisted a community documentation project and shared her
way of planning and plotting interviews, shown in the "Planning Grid"
sketch. (I first saw this rendered on a chalkboard by Mary.) In this case, the
community wanted to look at changing economic factors in the town, so they

groups of People / Perspectives

	Farm Families	Business People	Blue-Collar Workers	Service Members	Government Workers
The Depression					
World War II					
Main Factory Closing					
Vietnam War					
Farm Crisis (1980's)					
Recession (2000's)					
Oil Boom/ Bust (2010's)					

Time Periods of Subjects

chose to focus on peoples' jobs. The entries in the grid are not exhaustive of all possibilities—but they demonstrate the thinking behind a thorough planning process.

Always consider how the interview(s) will work with the broader library focus and collection—in what way can interviews be reflective of existing holdings, and to what advantage? Think about any resources that are highly valuable, in the sense of content versus dollars. Are those offerings (books, photos, maps, and databases) being fully explored? How might an oral history project add value to those offerings or become a portal into that content? Imagine a set of interviews that speak directly to the living experience of a location that is detailed on a historic map collection, or interviews with homegrown musicians, followed by a "did you know" statement that describes your database of streaming music. Oral history's benefit is not exclusive to the narrative of the recording. The contingent perk is an "aha" opportunity when participants realize more about your library's full set of offerings.

USING COLLABORATIONS AND PARTNERSHIPS

Despite your best imagination for what will be important to the community, and the priorities for developing your collection, relationships can be illuminating. If your library already is working with an organization or business, think about how your existing ties can be leveraged toward oral history. Maybe the outside group wants to establish its own interview set, and your location can be a landing spot for the work already in planning. Or, conversely, you might recognize that a business has deep local roots, and you can document that history—both for your library and as a service to that anchor in the community. You are creating new and pertinent information, and you are showing the library to be a progenitor of connections.

Once your library gains attention for its oral history work, people and organizations will seek you out to join forces on projects. The definition of collaborate says (1) **to work jointly with others or together especially in an intellectual endeavor,** and (2) **to cooperate with or willingly assist an enemy of one's country and especially an occupying force.**[7] Let's start with number two: Hopefully, your library does not have mortal enemies and is not squaring off against an occupying force. Nonetheless, libraries always are facing detractors and always proving their relevancy. Instead of rejecting or rebuking detractors, think of using oral history to demonstrate that the library exists for them. What are their critiques and concerns? Can those be addressed through oral history? How might their experiences be harnessed as information rather than opposition? Don't confuse collaboration with collusion (or pandering). The library does not endorse viewpoints but must be a place where opposing perspectives are shown.

Getting back to the first definition for collaborate: The key is to establish partnerships that are mutually beneficial versus independently exhausting; start with a shared understanding for how both parties are participating and gaining rewards. With oral history, the library is tapping a knowledge resource that is resident within a surrounding population. Even if that imperative is clear, the identification of where that knowledge resides might not be crystalline. You can lean on a sister organization, such as a historical society, to steer you to subjects that need exploring and individuals who can be part of a project. Your local humanities organization might be in tune with the critical conversations taking place in the community—the hot-button topics that need attending. Social service organizations will know who in the population is marginalized and for what reasons. The development of your collection comes from a comprehensive picture of opportunity, and you can work jointly with others to ensure that your vision is not myopic.

Establishing partnerships at the onset of a project means more attention to the outcomes. Automatically, you have agencies that will be positioned as your messengers and champions. Your mission is to facilitate knowledge creation, and the spread of your work must always find new outlets. In the age of digital content and worldwide platforms, *use* is the bridge to persistence: *Content survives because it is used.*[8] When you develop your collection jointly with others, the number of portals to the work is exponentially increased, and the future for additional relationships is being mapped.

THERE REALLY IS TREASURE EVERYWHERE

At our library's local history department, we once had a student stop by with a paper she had written about the history of the county and her analysis of its mythologies. It was a good paper, and after some back and forth, we decided to add it to our collection and create a catalog record for it.

A year or so went by, and she came back with another paper, this one on a major national political event. Since we had taken the last one, she wanted to see if we would be interested in this paper as well. The focus was national in scope, and didn't at first seem to align with our collecting interests, which were focused almost exclusively on the history of the county. Through discussion, however, we saw that this material was a bridge between local-county politics and the national scene; her father was a local politician who also was a national delegate. We looked more closely at the paper.

Interestingly, nearly all her citations were primary sources she had herself collected: oral history interviews conducted with many of the state delegates to the national convention. Together they formed a narrative of the convention from a hyper-local perspective. We asked whether she would consider donating them alongside the paper, and now we have a small but fascinating series of interviews that will undoubtedly be researched and allow people to better understand today's political climate.

By the time this student came by, the local history department had gone through several iterations of a documentation strategy, wherein specific community elements and/or sources are identified to be actively documented and/or collected. But this individual's ability to use her already deep connections in the community yielded information that would never have been captured using established systematic practices. Our communities are much more robust and complex than is capturable in any system. With that in mind, it is fair to argue that *any* investment in a relationship between the library and a community member is of value. The trick is to build the right kind of relationship.

Do your community members know that the library is a **repository** of local knowledge and that they can be **providers** of local knowledge, as well as consumers? Or, taking a step back, *is* your library a repository for local knowledge? If it isn't yet, it's good that you are reading this; continue building and make it so! And when you get there, reinforce this idea in conversations and interactions. As you are talking with patrons, add some elements to your regular reference interview geared toward learning more about them at a local level. You may find you are pulling new releases for the local barber, who knows everything about everyone, including where the gold is buried. You may find you are helping download tax forms for a former mayor, 30 years removed. Or a decorated veteran. Or a county planner. Every one of these community members has knowledge that could benefit current and future researchers. The library's role is to collect and disseminate this local knowledge; your job is to make sure that role is known to the community.

Adam Spiers

ENGAGING COMMUNITY

If I say "community engagement," what picture comes to mind? Do you see people walking in and out of the library? Asking questions at the reference desk? Checking out materials? What does *engagement* mean?

People come to the library—in person or online—to fill a gap between what they have and what they need or desire. Also, a library can proactively show people what they have been missing or what has escaped their awareness. Oral history is effective for presenting an array of understandings that don't exist elsewhere, experiences that otherwise go uncaptured. An additional and powerful aspect of oral history is its utility for showing people how they feel about themselves—for cultivating "self" identifications. Oral historian and writer Studs Terkel frequently spoke about the meaning imparted to the subject of an interview:

> His voice drops to a whisper as he recalls what it meant to people to be asked about their lives for the first time. "Oh, boy . . . yes, for the first book, I interviewed one mother of four little kids, skinny, pretty, bad teeth – meaning no dental care – and the kids are jumping around, 'cause they want to hear their mamma's voice played back . . . and so I play it back, and she listens to what she said on the tape and she says, 'Oh my God,' she says. 'I never knew I felt that way before.' " (Burkeman 2002)

The act of recording your own experiences, listening to yourself, and then listening to others in comparison is revelatory. And it's involving.

Participation and involvement define engagement. Developing a collection of interviews requires more than input and feedback; it demands work and creativity. As a librarian, you have ideas about what is important and necessary for pursuing in a project. At the same time, your members have a stake in the pursuant activities and they must jointly steer the process. What are their concerns, passions, and inclinations? Let them tell you what's important, and get them to help with the structure and organization of work to be done; collect their energy.

When you have subject matter that is complicated, expect to hear a range of views and experiences and understand that all appropriately coexist. The librarian's job is not to decide on any one truth; the role is to facilitate a conversation among and between competing voices. The existence of oral history interviews achieves this for you: Where multiple perspectives are offered side by side, in full and equal measure, those viewpoints speak to one another; the collection itself becomes conversant, and the collection *is* the community.

FINISHING THOUGHTS

Returning to the beginning of this chapter: The development of oral history comes from a place of imagination for what can exist; it is a process of creating what is not being offered through subscriptions, catalogs, or Amazon.com. Traditional collection development includes selecting new material from what is available and then replacing and weeding existing holdings; this isn't the case for oral history. Quite the opposite. A process of "thinning out" occurs before any interviews enter your library. At the inception of a project, you will calculate whom to interview, for what reasons, and how the content will enrich your library and community—into the future. Content grows in meaning through relationships, and your voices will increase in value throughout the years, as time and events cause members to listen and reflect on what has passed. Different aspects of the conversations will become important in ways you can't expect.

You can't predict the future. You can, however, recognize possibility and anticipate outcomes. The Western History Department of the Denver Public Library established an oral history collection focused on three overlooked neighborhoods called Globeville, Swansea, and Elyria. In 2017, Jim Kroll, manager of the Western History and Genealogy Department, agreed to discuss the aspects of that project. Jim's impressions are beautifully articulated, and his statements encapsulate what I am working to tell. Jim's reflections close this chapter and lead into the forthcoming chapters.

CN: So Jim, first, if you can give me some background about how the Denver Public Library first got involved with the Globeville, Elyria, Swansea community. And, from this point forward, I'll just refer to that as "the community." That's what you'll know—every time you hear that.

JK: In 2012, councilwoman Judy Montero contacted the library, wanting some photographs—old photographs—of the Globeville, Swansea, and Elyria neighborhoods. She was working with the community at that time to empower them to speak up, because the federal government and CDOT [Colorado Department of Transportation] were planning to do an expansion—or renovation, or replacement actually—of I-70 [Interstate 70]. . . .

And the next thing we started doing was collecting their stories, their photographs, at these townhall meetings that Judy was conducting with the neighborhood. That gave us some really good content, especially in the area of photographs. Then we decided we would use this material for an exhibit—an exhibit that we did around that same time, around 2013. It was in the Central Library; it was a place where, now, Judy could bring people from the community. And members of the community came on their own with friends and family to see these neighborhoods and to reflect upon what they were once like. . . .

Then, as we got to know the people who were part of Judy's group of advocates, [we] came to the realization that we could use some of these funds from the IMLS grant to conduct oral interviews. And those occurred in 2013.

CN: Now, I'd like for you to talk a little bit about how the oral histories enhanced or complemented or worked with the Denver Public Library collection on whole.

JK: Okay. We had received two IMLS [Institute of Museum and Library Services] grants. One was called "Creating Communities," which we focused on seven neighborhoods and put those up on our website. Then, the second grant was "Creating Your Communities," as I explained earlier, that it would be a way for people to upload and share their personal information.

So, we already had established that there were going to be, on our webpage, materials pertaining to the various neighborhoods—not all of the neighborhoods—in Denver. We are also very strong in the Department when it comes to just collecting neighborhood histories that have been published; helping people do the research on their homes or commercial properties that they own. Sometimes for sale purposes, more often just because they want to know the history of where they live, or where they work. This all tied into it quite nicely.

CN: What was—or, to what extent was there collaboration and outside help contributing, specifically, to the oral history project? So, outside of library staff.

JK: That gets back to Judy Montero and her staff. Judy helped us identify the people to be interviewed. Judy has a wonderful sense of diversity, so she made sure that the people we were going to interview represented a lot of cross sections of those three neighborhoods.

CN: And then, say a little bit more about the community participation—to what level the individual citizens participated. And what they might have gained from the overall project, outside of just being interviewed.

JK: Well, I think—using Judy's terminology if I can—they felt as though they mattered. They were singled out to tell their story, and tell their story that would be kept in a library, in perpetuity. That meant a lot to them. They had felt as though they were overlooked; that the government and the political establishment simply ignored them for all of these years. And yet, they were passionate and very dedicated to their neighborhoods.

NOTES

1. The parable of the blind men and the elephant has many versions and interpretations. I use the story to illustrate that individual truth is subjective. A broad perspective—accounting for other peoples' experiences—produces the most complete and accurate understanding.

2. A poetic explanation of oral history comes from historian Alessandro Portelli: "Oral sources tell us not just what people did, but what they wanted to do, what they believed they were doing, and what they now think they did."

3. In *Doing Oral History: A Practical Guide*, Donald Ritchie talks about the evolution of oral history. Ritchie's many references point to oral history being exercised by individuals from a variety of disciplines associated with universities or academia (typically).

4. The *Glossary of Archival and Records Terminology* does a magnificent job of explaining and distinguishing between terms that relate to archives and libraries and information science, more broadly. Though I don't identify as an archivist, I still love the *Glossary* and use it frequently for a variety of purposes. It's really cool!

5. In March 2012, a Colorado survey organized by the State Library showed that 96 percent of the state's reported oral histories are not fully accessible. Recognizing a national phenomenon, Nancy MacKay addressed the same point in the 2010 and 2016 editions of her book, *Curating Oral Histories: From Interview to Archive*.

6. Doug Boyd and Mary Larson, ed., *Oral History and Digital Humanities: Voice, Access, and Engagement* (New York: Palgrave Macmillan, 2014).

7. *Merriam-Webster's Collegiate Dictionary*. 11th ed. (Springfield, MA: Merriam-Webster, 2003).

8. I heard this discussed in a presentation that included representatives from National Public Radio, and it was repeated in an article from the newsletter of the Society of American Archivists: "Extending the Life of Stories," *Archival Outlook*, November/December 2011, p. 10. In that article, Tim Berners-Lee is credited as the source of the statement.

2

Record = Preservation

Ideally, the previous chapter ensured that you recognize the power, purpose, and value of oral history as a type of information and, especially, as a resource you want to pursue in your library. Also, you should see how "recognition" is akin to "collection development"—which is an active phrase, requiring you to do something. Being aware of oral history is the beginning; acting on that awareness is Step Two and is the focus of this chapter. This chapter takes you through major decisions involved with capturing interviews.

The concept of preservation is central to archival work and conveys special meaning. In the archival setting, preservation is the discipline of protecting materials/assets and minimizing damage; it's the act of "keeping from harm, injury, decay, or destruction." The archivist plays a guardian's role, mindful of future and posterity.[1] In a library setting—and specifically for oral history—the idea of "preservation" is no less important though less materially oriented. How do you preserve experience? How do you preserve community? How do you preserve individual truth? To preserve it, you must know it. Oral history is a means for achieving this kind of preservation—a snapshot of detailed knowledge conveyed through spoken expression. The librarian's role is to facilitate *this* preservation, recognizing the importance, and then making certain that the record button gets pressed.

CAPTURING VOICE

Hearing someone speak about his or her life, an event, or a topic—compared to reading the same—is impacting. And it's an interaction. The voice, as a vessel, has more content than a set of type or print words. This is not to suggest that written words don't have strength and energy. But think about it: As you are reading a letter, a poem, an essay, are you playing those words in your head? And if you don't know the voice, are you attaching a voice of your

imagination? This is called *identifying*. With a sound track you establish character and personality, grounding the script in something more distinct.

At the Boulder Carnegie Library, I have received messages from family members who came across recordings of their loved ones. Sometimes it's an individual who is generations removed from the voice that is part of our collection—maybe a grandchild who never met his or her relation. Invariably, the person has contacted me to convey how moved he or she is by the experience of hearing the grandmother for the first and only time. Through our recording, *she* has been saved; she is known. This is the power of voice. And this is the reason for letting people speak for themselves, through generations and into the future.

Format Options and Equipment

Within the oral history community, much discussion centers on the pros and cons of video versus audio recordings as a means of establishing "voice." The argument for video notes that people tell you much about themselves by the way they gesture with hands or show emotion through face—nonverbal expression. Also, you can learn about a person via choices made with clothing, jewelry, hairstyle, body art, and so on. In the same way that a transcript lacks the totality of a recorded conversation, the absence of visuals in oral history is a diminished package.

True: audio-only is a stripped-down form of recording. Also true: the absence of any distraction from what a person is saying can help deliver his or her message more effectively (no notice of that tuft of hair jutting from his ear or that stain on her blouse). Simply listening to a person allows full attention to the words, the intonations, and the emotions of the conversation. The experience of *just listening* turns out to be involving—the attendant listener places himself or herself into the verbal exchange and creates a mental map for navigating the topics of conversation.

Another option is to pair one or more photographs of the interviewee/narrator with an audio recording. Seeing the person—even if the visual does not come from the time of the oral history—can advance the relationship between the audience and the narrator. The narrator might have a picture that he or she particularly likes and considers a best reflection of identity. The photo might come from childhood or an occasion of significance. Or maybe the picture is not of the interviewee—maybe an object best conveys the character and personality of the individual. In self-selecting the image to be paired with the oral history, the narrator's presentation is individually determined and additionally meaningful.

While weighing the methods for capturing the oral history, equipment looms as a consideration. Without consulting a crystal ball, one point of certainty is this: In the future, the array of devices available—the choices for recording the oral history, either in video or audio—will be abundant. Any recommendation I might posture about a specific brand, model, or given device is bound to look sad and tired in ... five years? Two years? On the other hand, I can say with confidence that oral history always will demand crisp sound. So, in thinking about the equipment to match the direction chosen—audio or video—put sound as the highest priority. Does the recorder you choose allow for WAV files, which are uncompressed and, compared to MP3, superior in quality? What are you looking at in terms of microphones—built in or separate? Think too about the operation of the equipment—simple or complicated—and how that will impact the process as well as the final product. Will the person operating the equipment be competent and comfortable with the level of sophistication? Not intimidated? Will the narrator be comfortable, at ease, and uninhibited? The interview situation can be fraught and comes with its own burdens of detail in terms of preparation and execution; any means of simplifying the "stage" will benefit the product.

Lastly, ask yourself about the reasons backing up your ultimate decision. Are you following a trend? What are your resources for managing/maintaining the longevity of the equipment as well as the longevity of the final interview, be it a video or audio file? (Presuming "file" still is the word describing the containment of the interview, in this future scenario.) What is your vision for how the interview will be utilized—and what is the basis for this idea? Are you satisfying what you *think* is expected by a yet-to-be-known audience?

Remember that oral history is not done for entertainment; the purpose is to create information, which will assist in spreading knowledge to/in/through your community.

YOUR BIGGEST DECISION

The biggest and most important preservation decision is always, "What *exactly* do I want to preserve here?"

Going back to the source, you have to ask, what is it I'm documenting here? Your entire program design can hinge on this single, multifaceted question.

For instance, if you want to capture a person's words, you may get by with a stenographer. To capture vocal qualities, you need to step up to at least audio recording. If you want to record cultural practices of communication or any nonverbal means of communication (NMC), video is essential.

Let's look at some NMC that may have bearing in your decision.

Iaroslav Pankovskyi, in his 2010 paper, *Nonverbal Means of Communication: Benefits for SLA*, lists "Adornment; Chronemics; Haptics; Kinesics; Locomotion; Facial expressions; Oculesics; Olfactics; Paralanguage (Silence, Sound symbols, Vocalics); Posture; Proxemics."[2] That's a lot of linguistic terminology!

Much of Paralanguage and Chronemics (strategic use of time through pauses, waiting, etc.) will be captured in an audio recording, and you can get a fair amount of table swatting Haptics and other noises if you aren't careful, so let's focus specifically on what *can't* be heard.

Adornment such as clothing, jewelry, or even hair style, as mentioned elsewhere in this book, can be captured through still photography, presuming that all meaningful pieces are readily camera visible.

Kinesics and Facial expressions are probably the nonverbals you are most familiar with, Kinesics include hand waving, shrugging, nodding, and other gestures. Facial expressions include frowning, smiling, ruffled brow, and so on from what we all learned in primary school, but Oculesics is specific to the eyes and includes winks, closed eyes, wide-open eyes, and other eye movements. Imagine a narrator closing his or her eyes and talking about an event. Are there visual clues to a memory they are accessing? Is that meaningful to the researcher? Or only to the interviewer as a clue to draw out more of those clues or further develop the context of the memory? Perhaps it indicates speech well-rehearsed? Does the interviewer here interject to ask, "You are closing your eyes; what does that mean?"

Locomotion, Posture, and Proxemics are closely related, in that all relate to the placement of the body in space. Locomotion is not often a part of a formal sit-down interview, unless the narrator jumps up and starts pacing or runs out of the room! Posture and Proxemics, however, deal with how the narrator is arranging himself or herself in his or her space. Some "posture" is just habitual, such as my terrible slouch. However, after a certain period sitting, my slouch causes back pain and I straighten right up out of sheer self-preservation. This is reactive, and there are a ton of reactive postures. However, if the narrator turns away from the interviewer while relating something, this is venturing into Proxemics, how a person makes use of his or her personal space.

Each of these elements can greatly affect how an ambiguous statement can be resolved or add a layer of meaning to an already clear statement. It can be advantageous to train an interviewer to catch and resolve ambiguities when possible and reflect layers of meaning for confirmation. Of course, that is a trained skill set that you may not have access to. How does this affect your decision?

Adam Spiers

Participants Identified

Whose Voice?

Think back to the planning grid in Chapter One: That example demonstrates a strategy for establishing the types of people whose voices would be sought for a particular collection project. In selecting narrators, the first "must" is a possession of specific experiences that will lend to new understanding in an area targeted by the library along with the community. The second "must" is the ability to convey the details of that experience in a way that honors personal truth and dignity. The fact that a person possesses a story does not mean that he or she is capable of sharing the details. At all stages in life, memory fails—and with age, the energy for extended conversation also might be compromised. A selected narrator must be able to represent a perspective *and* himself or herself in a way that won't be erroneous or cause embarrassment. Again, as discussed in Chapter One: The librarian's role is not to decide on what is true; however, the librarian can confirm the presentation of personal honesty in a manner consistent with how the narrator would like to be remembered.

Whether you are building a collection of *life* interviews or *topic* interviews, a means for contacting potential narrators must be determined. The immediacy of a large-scale event—often, unfortunately, something traumatic like a tornado or act of social violence—will catalyze attention and interest from the community. You must be ready to receive names and contact information for people who are candidates for interview. This could be a simple spreadsheet, including the best means for reaching a person, how that person came to your attention, the experience(s) that are unique to the individual, and the date when the individual first presented as a candidate. You might advertise that you are accepting names—your library website, the community newspaper, or social media. Be careful, however, to avoid setting expectations for the promise of an interview. You should have a comprehensive pool of candidates and evaluate who is the best match for the needs of the project.

Be transparent about the process and the protocols for selecting individual participants. The community must know that each person is equally valued, even when all people can't be interviewed. Explain the limitations of library resources, the parameters that guide your decisions, and the anticipated outcomes for the interview or project. More than one person should share responsibility for picking interviewees—this helps skirt the appearance of prejudicial decisions.

Finally, even when you have laid a careful groundwork for drawing the most advantageous candidates, a pre-interview conversation is needed. This will be the opportunity to confirm that an individual does in fact have the breadth of experience and command of detail required for producing a substantive interview. Again, try to convey that an early conversation does not mean that a recorded oral history definitely will happen. Explain that, in the process, many people are contacted and not everyone is interviewed (owing to limited resources, time constraints, availability of interviewers, etc.). And if backing away from an interview proves too awkward, for whatever reason, by all means conduct the oral history—and keep it brief. Remember that your larger objective is to demonstrate the importance of community, community experience, and community voice. An unwanted interview still can have good consequence—as long as the narrator is competent.

Who Does the Interview?

The national Oral History Association has produced and periodically updates principles and best practices.[3] These statements outline the obligations and understandings that are inherent to the responsible exercise of oral history. The guidelines do not tell you who should or should not be an interviewer; however, they do contain clues as to who would be skilled at the methodology, based on what is principally and practically required.

A good interviewer knows how to ask open questions framed around Who, What, Where, When, How, and Why; understands that the narrator is the "hero" in the interview and should be the one doing most of the talking; practices active listening, fully engaged and prepared to be changed by what the narrator has to say; is comfortable with silences, when a narrator needs time to reflect or gain composure; and is able to conclude an interview when fatigue is evident. These are a few of the many, many skills/techniques that create a favorable climate for interview conduct. Other books and tutorials provide much more detail and wisdom about this aspect of oral history.[4]

With projects that focus on a topic or subject area (such as World War II or the Hippie Movement in the 1960s), interviewers can be either "insiders" or "outsiders." Think about interviews with nuns who are part of a religious order established in the community, interviews with miners whose life experiences are part of a past landscape, interviews with architects who have made significant contributions to the built environment, and interviews with bus drivers who have been working in the regional transportation system. In each example, a type of population is the focus of the interview, and the person doing the interview either will or will not be part of (or familiar with) that population.

Pros and cons accompany both instances. Someone who is part of the target population would have existing rapport, would know about important topics, and would understand idiosyncratic words and terms. On the other hand, a good interviewer is an advocate for the outside community and is an advocate for the future. Being part of the population might pose a barrier to asking candid questions, and if words/terms already are familiar, the interviewer might not ask for clarifications, which is what a general audience would need. The best scenario is one where a person knowledgeable about the population, with easy rapport, is trained to be cognizant of the people who will encounter the oral history. An insider who is able to remain neutral and inquisitive—and is not prejudiced about people and topics that might surface—would be an ideal interviewer.

Library people—librarians and information professionals—have long been the start point for uncovering and delivering material that can improve the lives of their community participants. But how often are we the progenitors of same material?

> To become builders of oral archives librarians must add analytic skill to identify what is significant in our own times in order to define the appropriate scope for each oral history project they undertake. Librarians must also learn interviewing and recording techniques. If research librarians do not rise to this occasion, a rare creative opportunity will escape them. (Zachert 1968)

Martha Jane K. Zachert, in March 1968, realized the fertile path that could emerge from oral history work. While she identifies with research librarians, her provocation should be absorbed by information professionals in all settings, and particularly the public domain. Zachert makes the case for librarians as interviewers—that our training and mindset lend themselves most naturally to the task. "Librarians have a near-intuitive rapport with

other individuals that comes from long and intensive public service." Is she correct? Are *we* the ones to be the most effective interviewers for our communities? At the end of this chapter, you will find a list of self-evaluative questions that elucidate the characteristics of a high-quality interview.

Others to Involve¿

At a minimum, the oral history interview involves an interviewer and a narrator. But a small and intentional support cast also might be involved, if the situation warrants. For video interviews, a person trained on camera techniques (lighting, angles, focus, etc.) should prep and monitor the equipment—no interviewer should have his or her attention divided between the narrator and the lens of a video recorder. In some instances, an interpreter might be required—either to translate between languages or to assist with questions/responses if the narrator's hearing is compromised. Also, an individual to take note of place names, personal names, and topics/keywords would be helpful. The interviewer's first priority is attention to the conversation; looking down, even briefly, to make notes is problematic as well as distracting. After the interview, the spelling of names can be verified, and this will assist with transcript preparation (if that happens) as well as cataloging metadata. Same for keywords and topics.

All of this said, the most important consideration is the comfort of the narrator, along with the rapport between the two key players: interviewer and interviewee. The space between these two must not be compromised.

Staging the Interview

Options for where to situate an oral history can be wide ranging. For sound quality, the ideal setting is a small room, sealed from outside noise, absent of inside noise (clock ticking, refrigerator humming, cat mewling), and buffered with enough physical material—carpet, tapestries, and pillows—to reduce echoes. Realistically, this might be difficult to achieve, but it's a worthy goal. A small table for resting the audio recorder (for oral interviews) and for placing water vessels and typed questions/notes is helpful; also helpful is a wall outlet for plugging in or charging the recording device. These ingredients build the conditions for an optimal recording.

The Comfort of Home?

Planning an interview at the narrator's home can be complicated. On the one hand, the home is convenient for that person—and it may even be necessary if the interviewee has restricted mobility. Familiarity with the surroundings eases some of the tension that comes with an interview, and being with a narrator in his or her home adds a layer of understanding that can inform some of the questions and conversation. On the other hand, a narrator may worry about making a good impression and can become self-conscious about the setting.

The greater danger is the unpredictability of being in a home, where all variety of distractions and noise might occur, and human interruption can be difficult to manage.

Imagine a scenario where one spouse is being interviewed, and the other is expected to remain out of the picture. The temptation to "just listen" can lead to "just adding a few thoughts," to "just making a few corrections." In addition, the dynamic between the interviewer and the narrator is distinctly altered with the presence of spousal ears. In some instances, the narrator may be less forthcoming, and the added pressure on the person conducting the interview is palpable. For these reasons, a more controlled setting often is preferred.

The Benefit of Neutral Territory

As previously stated, a home interview has layers of unpredictability. Also, in the case of library interviews—where the library is initiating the project—going to peoples' homes incurs risk. To avoid any hint or circumstance of impropriety, consider a public location for the oral history. In fact, think about your own location for the interview. Many libraries have study rooms that can be reserved for blocks of time. And those small rooms, with basic amenities, may be ideal for the staging of an interview. Part of the impetus for an oral history project is the fostered relationship between library and community. What better way to advance that relationship than by bringing people to the library for the interview—an opportunity to showcase other happenings and holdings and demonstrate the placement of voice as a shared resource.

For some interviews, a compelling case can be made for staging the interview in a spot that has meaning to the content of the oral history. Picture an interview with a restaurant owner who is discussing the business of managing that restaurant; the idea of conducting the interview on site, to capture atmosphere, has merit. But with ambient sound, what starts out as charming quickly turns to grating. With an extended interview, a future audience wants to hear the exchange of words—not the rattling of dishes or din of background conversation. All of that noise becomes taxing and is competition for the dialogue of the interview. Consider starting the oral history in the milieu of a specific atmosphere, and then pause and move to a quiet, controlled area to finish the conversation. Your future audience will carry the imagery of the soundscape (yes, sound creates images) and apply it to the oral history interview.

BECOMING A STEWARD OF THE RECORDING

Stewardship: the careful and responsible management of something entrusted to one's care.[5]

Care, responsibility, trust, and management. Those are the ingredients that comprise a recipe for stewardship. Hopefully, the first one is easy, as you **care** deeply about the purpose for your project, the experience of your community, and the outcome for the oral history. You are involved and invested in the longevity of the information and the anticipation for spreading knowledge in your community. You want the voices of your members to be part of a lexicon of understanding, entirely unique to the local needs. If you don't care, stop right now!

Responsibility is a bit more difficult, as it means stepping up to the plate—being transparent about decisions, acknowledging the limitations of your human and library resources, and then moving forward. In the early part of this chapter, the topic of audio versus video was discussed, with brief mention of WAV versus MP3 for sound files. Now is the time for a collateral conversation: What is your capacity and comfort for dealing with the format you create? Do you want to be responsible for a video? *Can* you be responsible? Is audio, with known standards for file extensions, more your speed? (At the time of this writing, a wide variety of file extensions are plausible for video, with no agreed-upon standard.) Being responsible also includes awareness of your role as a change agent. You are embarking on a creative journey, contributing to something enduring that increases in value over time. Own it! This is a reason for excitement. You are clearing a path for the community to move down, in conjunction with the library. Responsibility is recognition.

And this is why you have the **trust** of your community. With a clear plan of articulated intentions, members can believe in the worth of your actions. Trust is not a promise of perfection; it is a commitment to follow through with shared plans and adjust course if necessary.

The remaining tenet of stewardship is **management**. The ability to skillfully direct the handling of a single oral history—or a project—is crucial to the success of the venture. This is the follow-through that garners trust and demonstrates care and responsibility. If you are managing a project, you will be responsible for scheduling, tracking, reporting, and documenting everything. You will oversee people and resources; you will ensure that time tables are observed. However, be careful to also manage expectations. Do not let the perfect be the enemy of the good. Repeat: *Do not let the perfect be the enemy of the good.* Possibly, and likely, you will encounter others who are doing oral history work, who have more resources and more expertise, and may seem to be doing "better." Do not be disheartened; do not drop your intentions. "Do what you can, with what you've got, in the place where you are."[6]

Release Forms

Regardless of what format is selected for your oral histories, and regardless of any decisions about how interviews eventually will be used and disseminated, a release form signed by the narrator absolutely is necessary. This document will explain the context for the interview—why it is being done, for what purpose, with what intended consequence or outcome (i.e., to be part of the library collection)—and will demonstrate the clear transfer/sharing of copyright between the interviewee and the library. Oral history interviews are creative works, similar to literature or art, and therefore subject to copyright. Ownership is jointly held between both the interviewee and the interviewer, as those individuals jointly created the product through their shared time together. Both the narrator and the interviewer must sign a consent/release stating they approve of the library placing the interview in the public domain, to be used as the library deems appropriate for education. The wording on the release also should state that the narrator is permitted to do whatever he or she wishes with the original recording. Make clear that the product is not being given away—it is being shared.

Some people question whether a narrator would want to sign a release form, especially when the intent is to make the interview publicly accessible. Naturally, each interviewee will have different feelings about this; but what is the interview worth if it can't be shared? Aim for broad dissemination, for the specific reason of search and discovery. Remind narrators of the importance of their experience, their story, their voice, and their message— the reason for doing an interview is to expose others to the truth of firsthand knowledge. *Telling* is a form of power, and being heard is a confirmation of the story. As a legal document, the consent/release may intimidate some, but it demonstrates that the library takes seriously the responsibility of transforming individual story into shared knowledge.

Documentation

The oral history itself is a primary source and the focus of an interview project. At the same time, consider the merits of the surrounding information, which provides context for the circumstances of the interview. Content does not spontaneously create itself; someone, prompted by something, conceives of a project. The motivations, preparations, decisions, and executions all become reflected in the content. This is true for a library as progenitor, just as it's true for an individual author. Tracking decisions, tracking process steps, and tracking workflows—all of these documentary actions add to and extend the life of your interviews. If you clearly document activities, you will be able to look at what was done, understand the reasons behind decisions, and evaluate the choices made.

Good record keeping also will position your library for future success and for funding. As you hit your stride and start building collections, your ambitions may very well grow. Perhaps you envision a project where you'd hire a professional photographer to capture portraits of your narrators; your idea is to create a virtual exhibition that brings together oral history with portraiture, showing a diversity of faces and perspectives. You don't have the money to pay a photographer, but you know of a grant opportunity. Every granting agency wants to be told how an idea came about, how it will be executed, and how the results are ensured—a repetition of tested methods. Having taken the time to observe and record previous decisions and actions, you will be able to support your concept and the plan for execution.

Lastly, as you consider the preservation of process (a.k.a., "documentation"), remember that information about each and every interview will help build your eventual catalog records, which in turn will make your content accessible. Have a simple template for capturing the facets of information—or data points—that will make your interviews understandable to an outside world. At the time of an interview, establish names, dates, places, and so on, as they are relevant to the story of the oral history. Preservation is not something to be applied after the fact of the interview; it's not a clear wrapping. Preservation is an ongoing, iterative component of the oral history life cycle, and it is central to stewardship.

File Structuring

This book presumes that the medium used for capturing the oral history will be digital, and the file created will be electronic. Electronic holdings require special consideration, starting with a naming convention. No formal standard exists, though many universities and institutions offer guidelines.[7] The variety of approaches demonstrates the importance of local consistency and local applicability—meaning, your system for naming the files must meet your library's needs. The conventions must be meaningful to you, because you will be responsible for finding and retrieving files. That said, the experience of others should be considered. Conventions should be informative. For the interview file, you need to at least include the narrator's name—last name and possibly first name. Probably, you also will want to include the date of the interview's recording. And if you plan to place the interview in your catalog, a unique reference number (call number) is needed. Adding a unique number to each interview file can be extremely useful: If you have multiple interviews with one person, the separate oral history experiences quickly can be distinguished. In thinking about call-number assignment, be sure to allow much more collection growth than you anticipate requiring. With the above suggestions, a file might be named: **OH0001_Nelson_20170401 .wav**. This would be the first oral history in a collection not expected to exceed 9,999 interviews; the narrator's last name is Nelson, the interview was conducted on April 1, 2017, and the file is WAV format. Generally, you'd want to keep the file name at 25 characters or less, with no blank spaces—the underscores create visual separation.

The next consideration is a system for organizing all of your oral history files, with folder designations and hierarchy. You have choices about how to structure a system—again, the key is to forecast future needs and plan for the expedient retrieval of files as needed for presentation or duplication or other use. Remember: For each oral history, you will be generating more than just an interview recording; you will have release forms and data sheets, and you may have photos, transcripts, summaries, and so on. Each type of contributing material should be placed in a separate folder, and your file-naming convention should allow for the independent ingredients to be collated. Continuing with our example of the Nelson interview, a scanned copy of the release form might be named **OH0001_Nelson _Release** and reside in a folder called "OH Release Forms." A digital photo of the narrator might be called **OH0001_Nelson_Picture1** and reside in a folder called "OH Images."

With the contributing materials in separate folders, distinguished by file type, you might want to also have a single folder for every oral history, containing all of the components of that single interview. You can accomplish this by creating "shortcuts" to the original documents and collating all of those shortcuts into a single folder called "OH0001 Nelson." This way, you are not doubling the storage use, and you are not creating multiple versions of items that might require updating. The primary component of each and every oral history is the recording file, so careful management of that precious, unique ingredient is your primary concern.

Continuity of Collection (LOCKSS)

In 2008, I signed up for a digital preservation workshop, during which I expected to learn of a new system for ensuring that oral history files remained safe ... forever. Literally, I think I believed that "forever" existed—and I just needed to purchase this new LOCKSS product (the workshop advertised that we would learn about LOCKSS) in order to safeguard my oral histories. I was very sleepy for the start of the session, because I had spent the previous 36 hours riding a train across half of the United States in order to be at this very spot of coordinated enlightenment. The presenters started by talking about file types that are recommended for preservation quality (i.e., WAV) and about the dubious durability of CDs and DVDs (i.e., "gold" is a color, not an insurance policy). Then I might have napped a smidge, because suddenly we were deep into LOCKSS, and several individuals who were sharing this system were describing their experience. I kept waiting to hear details about who made LOCKSS, where it could be purchased, for what cost, and so on. And what did it look like? Was it bigger than a bread box? *Why were the relevant details being withheld?* Finally, my blurry attention landed on a handout with the word LOCKSS, and in parentheses: **Lots of Copies Keeps Stuff Safe.**

Can I tell you how happy I was to discover that I had paid for 1,444 miles of jostling, 36 hours of confinement, and 2.3 minutes of actual sleeping in order to learn: Keeping 17 identical pairs of shoes is the best way to ensure that you will be able to walk in that variety of shoe on any given day. (Insert your own "Picture of Happiness.")

> Keeping 17 identical pairs of shoes is the best way to ensure that you will be able to walk in that variety of shoe on any given day.

The best advice money can buy: Lots of Copies Keeps Stuff Safe. And stuff, in this case, is your oral history collection. However, having lots of copies is not enough. Let's go back to the example of the shoes: If all 17 pairs are tidily stacked in a closet that becomes engulfed in flames, your noble efforts have resulted only in a more expensive fire. So, as you think about a file system and electronic storage, consider a multiplicity of copies, a diversity of locations, and a stability of placement.

Ideally, you will have some storage that gets regular backups. That would be a spot for preservation copies, which are uncompressed files that you intend to *not* touch—unless you absolutely must. You would make a copy of that original file, and from *that* copy you'd make derivative files (e.g., MP3), which you can use for sharing and manipulating. Electronic files are at greater risk with each touching, when corruption might be introduced or transfer-error might occur.

Placing preservation copies—the ones not to be touched—on DVD or CD (even gold) should not be your choice. Those shiny discs may look durable, and seeing them lined up may feel like security, but that option simply has not born out for digital preservation. You don't really know what's happening with those discs—if they are holding up or degrading. And if your whole collection required retrieval, due to an electronic storage catastrophe, do you want to be going back to a shelf and pulling off discs, one by one, and then reloading those files onto a computer for use? Would your "computer" device even have a slot for CD/DVD? The more expeditious and practical path is to use a mass storage container (external drive? cloud space?) for all files. Then, be sure that you always are working off of copies made from the original, preservation recording—which has been separated and placed in your most reliable mass-storage option.

DIGITAL PRESERVATION OPTIONS

If you don't have a certified trustworthy digital repository, and your library has no immediate plans to build one, there are still many storage options to consider when developing out an oral history collection that is primarily born-digital. Which one is best for your library depends entirely on your particular needs accounting for what resources you already have available to you.

What do you really need?

- A safe place to put things
- A plan to maintain those things over time
- A good way to access them

Let's look at the first. Using LOCKSS as a jumping-off point, consider what storage space you have available to you locally, and then check to see which cloud services you can take advantage of.

There are as many storage options as there are types of libraries. At some institutions, you may just ring up the IT help desk and start your way down the path to providing public access to your well-protected digital assets. Other institutions may be competing for resources and need to shoestring prototypes while building the business case for increased funding. Whatever your situation, there are options.

If you or your IT department has a sophisticated setup, you may feel more comfortable hosting everything internally. If this is the case, you should have a candid conversation with your IT support team, in which you include myriad "What Ifs," such as:

- "What if there is a tornado or flood that wipes out our servers?"
- "What if someone clicks on a bad email link and everything is ransomwared?"

These are unfortunately serious questions with serious implications for whether your unique materials will survive common catastrophes. Take it a step further, ask "What happens if the hardware fails?" or "What happens when you get a better offer at a different library?" to probe some very common issues that can all too easily turn out to be catastrophes. If you don't like the answers, or don't even feel comfortable about the answers, plan for inevitable disaster and continue having the conversation—as the steward for your materials, it is your responsibility to make sure they are safe.

If your local storage is a single server or external drive, or if you have no space yet at all, you will need to consider some sort of cloud storage option. You want to have lots of copies to keep your stuff safe and the cloud is a great place to do that.

The bigger household name companies (Google, Microsoft, DropBox, and Amazon) provide several GBs of cloud storage for free, or 50–100s of GBs for tens of dollars annually. Not bad for a redundant copy of your preservation files, if your collection is relatively small or in a proof of concept phase.

You could also consider using the Internet Archive at archive.org. If your copyright/licensing agreements align with the Internet Archive, you can post your audio or video files there, and they will be available so long as the Internet Archive is. They also seem to have no limits on how much you can put there, so long as it is open access.

Looking through your options, keep an exit strategy in mind to avoid decision paralysis. If you can easily export your content from it, you can change your mind later when your needs change.

Adam Spiers

FINISHING THOUGHTS

This chapter on preservation will likely receive sharp criticism for the many things I do not suggest, that would be found in comprehensive training for archivists. I do not want any librarians to be discouraged from working with oral history because they fear the demands of maintaining files, or fear they won't create the "correct" type of file, or won't have the layers of preservation strategy that characterize Trustworthy Digital Repositories.[8] The truth is this: Librarians engaging with oral history are dealing with realities—in work patterns and priorities—that don't match conditions that govern archival settings. The placement of resources and the emphasis simply are different, because the mission is different. The librarian's mission is more about sharing and facilitating, versus keeping. Librarians must lean on the strength of *our* guiding principles, *our* training, and seize the opportunities that our vision can bring.

Oral history fulfills its prophecy only when the story contained within reaches an audience. For the story to be preserved, it must be passed on. Librarians can work with community to create the space for individual truth to be expressed and received. We can utilize our systems for describing, organizing, and disseminating information, in order to deliver the message of community voice. This can be our power.

NOTES

1. Richard Pearce-Moses, *A Glossary of Archival and Records Terminology* (Chicago: Society of American Archivists, 2005), pp. 304–305.

2. Iaroslav Pankovskyi, *Nonverbal Means of Communication: Benefits for SLA* (Przemyśl, Poland: Nauka I studia, 2010), pp. 31–44. https://web.archive.org/web/20170816215854/http://www.rusnauka.com/15_APSN_2010/Pedagogica/67098.doc.htm.

3. The national Oral History Association's *Principles and Best Practices for Oral History* document is available through their website: http://www.oralhistory.org/about/principles-and-practices/.

4. Donald Ritchie's editions of *Doing Oral History* include insight about the interview process. Also, the national Oral History Association maintains a list of web guides for doing oral history: http://www.oralhistory.org/web-guides-to-doing-oral-history//.

5. *Merriam-Webster's Collegiate Dictionary*. 11th ed. (Springfield, MA: Merriam-Webster, 2003).

6. This quote, with slight variations, seems to be nearly universally attributed to Theodore Roosevelt, though it may just have appeared in his 1913 autobiography. Arthur Ashe shared a similar sentiment with: "Start where you are, use what you have, do what you can."

7. The Oral History in the Digital Age website contains more than one article relevant to file naming, such as this one: http://ohda.matrix.msu.edu/2012/08/file-naming-in-the-digital-age/. Perhaps more useful, reference is made to universities that publish different approaches to file naming (Michigan State University, Indiana University, and University of Wisconsin). Bear in mind, these are not specific to oral histories but applicable to all digital objects.

8. According to OCLC, a Trustworthy Digital Repository is one "whose mission is to provide reliable, long-term access to managed digital resources for its designated community, now and in the future." A framework for this mission is offered through TRAC, *Trustworthy Repository Audit and Certification Criteria*. As one would expect, a high bar is set for establishing this kind of system.

APPENDIX: WOULD YOU MAKE A GOOD INTERVIEWER?

1. Do you understand that the spotlight is not on you?
   - *Your job is to entice the narrator's story. Limit your own remarks.*

2. Do you know how to ask **open questions**?
   - *Avoid inquiries that are answered merely with yes or no.*
   - *Engage the narrator with topics that require thoughtful recall.*
   - *Frame questions around Who, What, When, Where, Why, and How.*

3. Can you ask one question at a time?
   - *The narrator may lose focus if you pose more than one inquiry in the same question.*

4. Do you practice brevity?
   - ** The ideal exchange entails brief questions followed by lengthy replies from the narrator.*

5. Are you sensitive to uncomfortable topics?
   - *Prepare for this eventuality; this is part of your responsibility.*

6. Do you understand timing?
   - *You need to know when/how to approach delicate topics.*

7. Can you weather silence?
   - *Sometimes a narrator needs time to collect his or her thoughts. Patience is a virtue!*

8. Can you weather your own fumbles?
   - *Sometimes your questions won't sound polished. This is natural.*

9. Are you an active listener?
   - *Eye contact tells the narrator that you are paying attention.*
   - *Good listening means that you are prepared to be changed by the narrator's comments.*

10. Are you willing and able to depart from a prepared guideline?
    - *Don't interrupt a good story.*
    - *Don't feel obligated by a list of specific questions—have a list of topics.*
    - *Pursue questions that arise from a pertinent story.*

11. Do you know how to pull a narrator from the abyss of a rambling tangent?
    - *Encourage the narrator in a preferred direction.*
    - *Don't be dismissive—but do be helpful.*

12. Can you elicit full descriptions?
    - *A mental image may cue a whole picture; include all senses.*

13. Can you distinguish between eye-witness experience and secondhand testimony?
    - *Ask questions that will place the individual at or apart from a scene.*

14. Are you able to refrain from confrontation?
    - *Your job is not to challenge or establish accuracy; you are establishing a perspective.*

15. Can you tactfully discuss discrepancies?
    - *Mentioning other perspectives is appropriate.*

16. Will you hold your ground when necessary?
    - *A narrator may want a third-party in the room; usually a bad idea.*

17. Will you know when (and how) to wrap up the interview?
    - *Watch and listen for signs of fatigue—best to stop at two hours.*
    - *Set a date for a second interview if need be.*

18. Are you willing to evaluate your work?
    - *Listen to the interview! Take every opportunity to improve your technique.*

19. Are you able to digest imperfection?
    - *No interview will be flawless. Live and learn.*

20. Will you follow through with postinterview processes?
    - *All your hard work amounts to SQUAT if consent forms aren't signed.*

3

Represent = Organization

As discussed, the construction of this book is centered on four Rs that progressively work to transform individual story into shared knowledge. You have come to the third R in the sequence, and this chapter might be the most dynamic, charged with possibility and also peril. The exciting possibility is that, through efforts to expose and explain the nature of any given interview (a.k.a., organize and represent it well), you enable the connection to a future audience. The scary part is that no single roadmap exists for arriving at that target destination. And, too, with exposure comes risk. At the time of this writing, some in the oral history community are ringing alarm bells about making interviews widely accessible—for the reason that, with oral history, the object of revelation is an actual person (not an object). Personal details naturally are revealed through the course of a thorough interview, or in the process of describing an interview. The fear of negative repercussions—or unintended consequences—is real. If a person describes a traumatic incident, how will that impact the way that others perceive them in the future? Will they be judged?

Sensitivity and thoughtful awareness must always accompany oral history. At the same time, the purpose and power of the interview is achieved only when the message is heard, when the content is received. Believing that oral history has the potential to deeply inform community understanding of people, topics, and ideas, and believing that individuals deserve to share their voices, the library is obliged to use every tool in its disposal to represent the interviews that come from engagement with oral history.

CREATING ACCESS POINTS TO THE AUDIO

In *The Organization of Information*, Arlene G. Taylor suggests that one primary reason for why we organize is a need to *understand*.[1] Imagine the

situation where a complicated idea is being presented, and as a listener, you are stretching to grasp the meaning or significance of what you are hearing. You need guideposts to move you from one point to the next; you need context for statements, to picture the correlations. Maybe you achieve this by taking time to organize your own reactions and interpretations, or maybe the presenter needs to improve the delivery of the content, offering better explanations and evident relationships.

When you offer materials to the community, you do so by explaining attributes of the holdings, in order for members to decide whether or not a particular item will meet the needs of the inquiry. You attempt to create a detailed picture that will facilitate understanding. Remember the anecdote in Chapter One, where the separate individuals, unable to see the whole elephant but touching different parts, come to distinct conclusions about what they are encountering. In that example, if the characters had been told they were feeling some part of an elephant—presuming a familiarity with elephants—they likely would have known exactly what they had in hand. Now let's switch the picture: Imagine that you are walking in the park and find a small slip of paper—a fortune. The fortune says: "Soon you will encounter a trunk." Specific, right? Or not so. Maybe the trunk you have in mind is like a big suitcase (how exciting!). But what about the trunk of a car? Is the fortune predicting that you will be stuffed into a hatchback? (Boooo!) And then, there's the elephant in the room. . . .

Surrounding information is crucial to understanding even the most specific detail. The more context you provide, the more touch points you create, which is vital to bringing shape to something abstract like "oral history interview." Consequently, the community will be better able to discern and appreciate the content you are offering.

Transcription

At its most basic, transcription is the process of transferring data from one recording format to another. This can be "an arrangement of a musical composition for some instrument or voice other than the original."[2] And, in the case of oral history transcripts, it is an effort to copy something aural to something textual. The relevant point—which is explicit in *Merriam-Webster's* definitions—is that all forms of transcription are representations.

Why Transcribe

Among oral history practitioners, discussion has ensued as to the justification and appropriateness of offering transcripts for interviews when a recording is available.[3] Consensus is that the audio or audio/visual presentation contains layers of meaning not possible to convey through a textual rendering. And when a transcript is present, an audience might favor that medium over the recording, never choosing to listen—which means that information is lost. This is a frustrating conundrum, especially for professionals who are in the business of pushing information. More is better.

Thinking about an oral history of duration 75 minutes, how is it possible to explain the full content of that interview? How is it possible for a potential listener to comprehend what is contained, in order to *want* to pay attention? I recall a specific comment from an archives practitioner, stating that he was tempted to suppress the existence of transcripts in order to force researchers to listen to the interviews in his collection. And while that approach would be extreme, the intention is understandable. Reality, however, tells us that "it is idealistic and naïve to think users can effectively discover specific information in interviews without the assistance of a transcript or an index" (Boyd 2014, 84).

> The key is to concretely define and explain the transcript as an assisting device and not a primary record.

The key is to concretely define and explain the transcript as an assisting device and not a primary record. The transcript allows a researcher to view the entirety of an oral history interview, to literally see the duration. Most interviews cover a range of topics that meet the objectives of the conversation; a family member may be interested in the entirety, but a researcher likely will be attentive only to portions. The transcript allows a researcher to scan the oral history and identify parts that are relevant to his or her query. Those segments then can be explored in the recording. As a value-added benefit, observing the placement of those segments allows the researcher to see what brought the narrator to the point of sharing that information. Context is visually offered via the transcript. And notably: Along the way of looking for specific nuggets, the searcher might come across other information that is surprisingly helpful or interesting. This is like scanning a bookshelf for a given title, only to find your attention snared by the surrounding spines.

A final thought, casting back to the archivist who was tempted to withhold transcripts in order to motivate his audience to listen: With so much information available on any given topic, at any given time, and in so many packages of delivery, an oral history absent of an accompanying transcript might be deliberately skipped; it might feel like too much work, compared to other more explicable resources. That would be the worst scenario pulled from a shelf of possibilities.

Nuts and Bolts—And Art

At the time of this writing, automated speech-to-text technology is rapidly advancing. Options exist for paying to have a sound file translated into a block of words—with many/most of the words matching what was spoken.[4] With oral history, the difficulty resides in the variety of speech patterns, volumes, accents, dialects, and general expressiveness that muddles with technology's desire for predictability. Even with the finest software/service money can buy, portions of the resulting transcript will be comically wrong. But the interest in this field surely points to a future where aural is mechanically (magically!) rendered textual with good accuracy.

Yes, technology can turn speech into displayed words—still, you would have good reason to employ a human to do the work, to create a product that is more faithful and more easily absorbed. Humans have the discernment to construct sentences, add appropriate punctuation, and break the narrative into digestible paragraphs. Humans can make note of vocal outputs like laughs or sighs—or pauses where the narrator is demonstrating hesitancy or stretching to find the correct words. These layers make a transcript more informative to the reader's eye and can help push the reader toward listening.

Transcription is a time-intensive and mentally demanding activity. It requires patience and diligence; it is not something just anyone is suited to undertake. That said, the idea is straightforward: Type what you hear. And tools exist to help with that process. A person can use software to slow the speed of the spoken conversation, to view time elapsed (for adding time stamps), to set up hot keys for stopping and starting the audio file—or for using a foot pedal to stop and start the audio.[5] The available applications don't do the work for you, but they can ease the strains of the task. Adding time stamps to a transcript is imperative—every couple of minutes, at least,

Beware Automated Voice Translation

and ideally with every change of direction in the flow of the narrative. The need for time stamps will be more evident in the next chapter's discussion of functionality.

If you will be transcribing a quantity of interviews—as part of a large project or as an ongoing component of your library's collection—you would benefit from *style guidelines*. Guidelines establish consistency in the end product: They can explain why and when to add time stamps; they can instruct technique and formatting, along with the basics of punctuation. You might refer to or pull from existing standards like the *Chicago Manual of Style*—though much of oral history transcription is subjective and artistic, rather than rules based.

The central idea, of course, is to accurately repeat the words spoken by both the interviewer and the narrator. Beyond that, you can make decisions about how much to repeat—as in, do you type every *um, uh, ah,* or *mm*? And what if the narrator is talking and the interviewer is simultaneously making empathetic remarks like *yeah* or *uh-huh*. A transcriber quickly learns that people in conversation make false starts (e.g., "I went to the—based on his recommendation, I stopped by the market.") and don't speak in perfect sentences. Conversations are fluid, with one thought stringing into another thought, punctuated by *and* or *so* rather than period, comma, or semicolon.

The approach to transcription should be guided by the utility that is intended. I have suggested that a transcript be used as a support document, to help researchers see and understand the content of the oral recording. In a best effort to represent what is heard, a transcriber could omit habitual fillers like *um* or *ah*. These verbal outputs lend no meaning to what is being discussed and get tuned out by our ears at the time when we are involved in the conversation (provided they don't occur with such frequency as to be utterly irritating). The next time you are talking with someone, pay attention to the phenomenon of fillers, false starts, and fluidity; notice the difference between what you are absorbing as information compared to the entire stream of words that comprise the exchange.

If our ears tune out fillers, the opposite is true for our eyes. Reading a transcript that includes all of those, *like*, interjections can be jarring, *you know*, if not torturous—especially for the person who was doing, *like*, the speaking and now sees, *you know*, his or her remarks cast into text. The written word, as we experience through published materials, is calculated and polished. People may wish that they spoke with such tidy construct; rarely is that true. Instead, people speak with personality. Reflecting again on what's useful about having a transcript, the researcher navigating the text does not benefit from seeing every *um* or *ah*, and calling attention to those verbal tics is unnecessarily distracting.[6]

> Invite the interviewee to review the transcript, to ensure its factual accuracy.

Lastly—and this gets to the point of the narrator's feelings about seeing his or her words—a best practice is to invite the interviewee to review the transcript, to ensure its factual accuracy (according to the narrator). Most oral histories include mention of person and place names, dates, titles, and so on. Having the interviewee look things over and correct misspellings or misheard details will improve the end product. Also, this is an opportunity for the narrator to confirm that he or she is comfortable with all that was said in the interview. Many people, reading their own words, are tempted to rewrite things to "sound" better. Explain that the transcript is not the equivalent of the oral history—rather, it's a tool for representing the content of the original recording and must remain faithful to that primary source. When people understand the big picture, they are likely to appreciate what is being accomplished.

TRANSCRIPT AS METADATA

Here's why transcription as metadata matters:

In 2013, I received a phone call from an out-of-state patron interested in ordering copies of an interview in our collections on CD. I thought we could work something out and inquired how many copies? Five? Yes, five, for each of the children of the interviewee. This was getting interesting. It turns out, this patron was the mother of a middle school student who had been charged with writing a report on World War II. This enterprising student knew her grandfather had served, and so went to googling the ship she knew he served on, to maybe find some pictures or other information. She searched her grandfather's name and the name of the ship, and lo, she found a two-hour interview with the grandpa that had been conducted by the library as part of the Veterans History Project.

It doesn't end there. Grandpa had passed away and had never talked with his family about his experiences during the war I was told, nor did he mention this interview. This veteran had 5 children, 14 grandchildren, and 2 great-grandchildren, and all listening for the first time to grandpa's stories about the war. Stories none of them had ever heard. Not once. Life-changing stories that perhaps, or more likely, change how they interpret their own past.

The transcript, as metadata, allows a much broader set of connections to be drawn than whatever limited set of subjects you could cram into a MARC (MAchine-Readable Cataloging) record. Imagine the granddaughter of a buddy of our veteran also googling around, learning that her grandpa, only briefly mentioned in the interview, saved someone's life amid chaos and horror. Or simply that he made powdered milk taste better in the field by adding a bit of cinnamon and vanilla. These interviews shed significant light on the realities of war and are studied in depth by professional researchers working to understand the effects of war. But they can also meet the hyper-specific needs of a single individual looking to connect with the past, if only we surface the metadata that allows them to do so, in the casual and effortless way that only the Internet can seem to conjure.

One more example: A local historical society conducted a fairly significant number of interviews in the 1990s. Each of those interviews focused on general life in the area, and each of those interviews touched on, to one degree or another, a major flood that occurred there in 1965. We were able to very quickly compile a very wide-perspective narrative through a simple key word search ("Flood") across our collections. What was great was that interviews surfaced where only a few seconds were devoted to the subject, not nearly enough to warrant a subject heading, that added very specific detail about sights and sounds of the disaster that painted a much more visceral picture than with just the few interviews where the flood was the focus.

So, how do you do this? Just put the transcript in a searchable format and make it available online. Let Google or Bing (or Ask Jeeves!) be your discovery layer. For instance, if you have web space for each audio file, consider having a PDF of the transcript made available online alongside the interview. If you can have the transcript embedded directly in a webpage as HTML, rather than in an object, it will surface in any search engine of choice. And if you have a digital asset management system that allows you to dump the whole transcript in a metadata field, that works too. Whatever your setup, just remember that getting the whole thing up is important. This will help you recover it too when you recall but can't quite remember which interview causally mentioned where the gold is buried.

Adam Spiers

Further Description

The transcript is incredibly powerful for demonstrating the content of an interview, and it can be imperative if a person is trying to piece together excerpts, to make use of the oral history for a reproduction of some sort. Still, the transcript itself does not describe the oral history. And an hour-long interview might produce a textual document of 15 pages, which is too lengthy to be useful for directing a researcher's initial attention. Something else needs to say, "Hey! Look at me!"

An alternative—or supplement—to the transcript is a well-constructed summary/index, formatted with time stamps. After the fact of the interview, a listener can make note of what is being spoken, when, and indicate shifts in the direction of conversation. The summary is more expedient to create, compared to a transcript, and it does have the advantage of allowing "aboutness" description, where the listener applies an amount of analysis in noting what is being discussed. Of course, the same subjectivity that provides "aboutness" analysis could produce bias or omissions—so the pros and cons must be weighed.

Along with either summary or transcript, an abstract and a list of keywords/topics go a long way in showing what is contained in the oral history. Again, the point is to establish digestible facsimiles that direct researchers' attention, in the same way that journal articles or papers receive descriptive treatment. Any effort to place to the oral history into a position of reaching its audience is worth undertaking. After all, the giving and receiving of information—the connection—is the purpose of creating the interview in the first place. And this brings up metadata.

Metadata

> *We kill people based on metadata.*
> —General Michael Hayden, former head of the NSA

Summary, abstract, and keywords all convey information about an oral history. Metadata, too, is grounded in "aboutness," though at a higher level.

Arlene Taylor explains: "All information resources have some basic attributes in common, such as *title, creator, topic* ... collectively, these attributes are known as metadata." Simple, right? But conversations involving metadata can turn, rather quickly, into a plate of spaghetti. You start with something cut and dry (like a noodle in the box), and then you think about it, and think about it ... and soon the firm strands of understanding will soften, twist, and entwine, until your brain feels like a tangled pile. Let me attempt to keep things straight.

Metadata and *cataloging* sometimes get used interchangeably. But a distinction must be made: Catalog records contain metadata; catalogs organize records that contain metadata; cataloging provides rules for placing metadata into a structured schema. Catalogs, however, don't tell you WHAT information to capture—what is important to know.

When General Hayden invoked metadata, he was referencing the controversy over the National Security Agency's (NSA) practice of gathering phone records. The explanation was that NSA did not record actual talking—rather, they gathered information *about* the phone calls: numbers involved, time of call, duration of call, location of participants, and so on. And the accumulation of these data points was sufficient to warrant actions, apparently. So you see the significance of what we are dealing with. But just what *are* we dealing with?

The difficulty with metadata is in deciding which information points are going to be most relevant and helpful to the library as caretaker, to the public as consumer, and maybe to the narrator as creator. At the time of this writing, no standard exists for suggesting the elements that will prove most fruitful in making oral histories discoverable, understandable, available, and usable. But don't throw up your hands. Rather, apply your training and expertise toward this dilemma, knowing it can be solved—or at least addressed. Librarians can explore existing models for metadata content and how those applications might extend to oral history. The job is to structure your *thinking*, in order to identify (a) the traits that are common to oral histories and (b) the significance of those traits to the interview and to an outside audience.

One conceptual model for guiding thinking is the Functional Requirements for Bibliographic Records (FRBR).[7] FRBR emphasizes things, characteristics, and relationships. The starting point is a *work*, which is the existence of something intellectual or artistic. The work comes out in some fashion—is expressed. When that *expression* is captured, you have a product called a *manifestation*. Being the first concrete entity (did I mention that in FRBR all "things" are called *entities*?), the manifestation gets described in a catalog or database. But the entity that literally would be delivered to the public is an *item*. So, with oral history, the **work** is the set of memories or knowledge residing within the narrator. Those memories/experiences come out through an oral telling—the **expression**. When the expression is captured through either audio or video, that is the **manifestation**. But the **item** that gets shared and played is a file type: WAV or MP3, or MOV or MP4 or VOB, and so on.

Then, too, you have human entities who play some role in the creation or caretaking of the work, expression, manifestation, or item. These responsible actors would be individual *persons* (such as a narrator, interviewer, videographer, and transcriber) or *corporate bodies*, which are organizations of people (business sponsors, universities, and libraries). And finally, subjects of the oral history would be identified as *concepts*, *objects*, *events*, or *places*. FRBR goes on to articulate relationships among all these entities.

In introducing FRBR, my goal is to demonstrate that models exist for guiding and organizing your thinking about oral history metadata. All entities have attributes (metadata!), which are the properties and characteristics that facilitate discovery, identification, selection, and acquisition. Using the FRBR model, you have a comprehensive structure for viewing the facets of oral history: work, expression, manifestation, item; persons, corporate bodies; and concepts, objects, events, places. The next step would be to ask yourself: What is important to know about each of those facets? What will be most helpful to the public and to the library, to extend the life of the interview and make the content accessible?

While a standard for oral history metadata does not exist, discussions have reverberated in the oral history community, and more people are weighing the importance of this thought process.[8] Practically speaking, the job of the library is to imagine what will be helpful and plan the means for obtaining or creating those helpful access points:

- identifier/call number
- title for the oral history interview
- full name of both narrator and interviewer
- narrator date of birth
- narrator location of birth
- date of interview
- occasion for interview/project description
- location of interview
- duration of interview
- type of manifestation (audio or video)
- item type (MP3 or MP4)
- location of item (library/repository)
- copyright/terms of use
- associated concepts, objects, events, and places (content description)

The above is a sample set, illustrating the types of things that could be meaningful in connecting the interview with its audience. Oral history is different from other creative works—a novel, for example—where the expression can be digested and appreciated purely on its own terms. With oral history, an awareness for surrounding circumstance is crucial. Think of a time when you heard someone speaking, and his or her ideas and choice of words seemed shocking—fringe or anachronistic. Knowing when and where the person was born, and something about his or her age and upbringing, helps explain the origin of that person's perspective and helps connect the dots. Details that are not explicitly mentioned during the interview can tell a back story that is necessary for fully appreciating the recorded content. Metadata, when it comes to oral history, is essential not just for extending the life of the interview (e.g., noting file types, to plan the inevitable reformatting of content) but for establishing context that facilitates understanding.

WORKING WITH CATALOGS/INFO RETRIEVAL SYSTEMS

If we organize because we need to understand, we do so also because we want to obtain things that exist somewhere—we need to retrieve the entities that await our discovery and use.[9] In the previous section, the criticality of metadata was made evident. But the follow-up to *having* metadata is *doing* something with it—placing that information into structures that apply meaning and organization. When shopping for a countertop oven, you may be able to walk into a store and experience all of the models that are on hand, but your time is better spent exploring options in advance, to see if a trip is warranted. Maybe you have a catalog that was delivered in the mail, and you can peruse the selection of ovens, comparing your specifications to those of the listed models. Or maybe you use the store's website to observe depictions of ovens, creating advanced searches by selecting desired attributes and eliminating options beyond the scope of what you want/need (who needs to pay $400 for a toaster oven?). The relevant note: Something happened behind-the-scenes to make your catalog or online experience work well.

> If we organize because we need to understand, we do so also because we want to obtain things that exist somewhere—we need to retrieve the entities that await our discovery and use.

Bib Records and Items

Whatever retrieval system is in use for your library—OPAC, ILS, Content Management System, or Digital Asset Management System—try to ensure that oral history gets item-level attention. Each and every voice must be

individually represented through surrogate records; the access points that establish unique identification and context require dedicated treatment. Before inserting oral history metadata into a record such as MARC, think about how the fields are used for other types of resources, and try to mimic the desired result. Some fields are keyword searchable (summary) while others are used more as phrases (subject headings). Ensure that descriptive elements (abstract, topics, etc.) are advantageously aligned. Also, you might need to place a collating note—for example, "This interview is part of a collection known as the Hairy Bacon Project"—into a field that allows searching, so all interviews with shared provenance are brought together. Authority control is challenging with oral history, when people and topics can be extremely local and specific to the community. Your mandate is to exercise consistency: Decide on exact wording that describes a project, and think of keywords that will be broadly representative of content; repeat wording with each interview that is part of a project, and place wording consistently in the same fields. Work with your cataloging department to think things through—the library is a team, and every person in the library has a common goal of positioning information for discovery.

A template like MARC might not be perfect for oral history, but if MARC gets used in your library, take advantage of it. Surrogate information (a.k.a., metadata) can be placed into *any* template, schema, structure, or framework, as long as you capture the information and keep the logic of the information (e.g., "Narrator name: Nelson, Cynthia K."), and store the information in sheets that are independent of the cataloging system. Have a text doc for each interview, or have a spreadsheet. The record in a catalog does function to contain data points (when you store item-level records), but the flexibility of having an independent "information sheet" could be your bridge to the future.

Beyond Catalogs

Explaining the Semantic Web, linked data, or the Resource Description Framework (RDF) is beyond the scope of this book—which is convenient, because the ability to do so with competence is beyond the scope of my brain. That said, information searching, harnessing the full potential of the web, is headed toward these ideas and resources. Welcome this future, even if the underlying concepts are not yet familiar; the variety of means for connecting people and ideas exceeds the limitations of timeworn library cataloging. The Semantic Web envisions a delivery of data wrapped in meaning, eventually leading to understanding. Think of R. L. Ackoff's progression from Data to Information to Knowledge to Understanding to Wisdom, where layers of utility add to greater and greater capacity for human decisions and actions.[10] In Ackoff's model, "data" becomes "information" when *meaning* is applied—which precisely is the strength of oral history.

RAGE AGAINST THE SILO: LINKED OPEN DATA

Let's talk a little bit about Linked Open Data.

Does it matter how it works? Only a little bit, from our perspective. What is most important is that Linked Data is fast becoming the lingua franca of the Internet. It is how Google is talking to Wikipedia is talking to Internet Movie Database (IMDB) is talking to Amazon, and how your fridge will be talking to your phone and your thermostat and possibly the grocery store. It is why a search screen shows a book ready to buy (one click away from your doorstep!) right next to the usual results in your browser.

At base, Linked Data comprises a syntax: Resource Description Framework (RDF), populated with "words": Uniform Resource Identifiers (URIs). A Uniform Resource Locater (URL) is a kind of URI, and URIs are published to the web as open data sets. The computer "reads" the URIs in the context of the RDF statement to understand what is being said. Specific URIs allow, for instance, the computer to differentiate or contextualize the term "bronco," which could refer to a kind of horse, a member of an American football team, a popular Mexican Grupero band, or a model of vehicle manufactured by Ford.

Not all Linked Data is open. As of this writing, IMDB may be used for free in specific circumstances but is in fact copyrighted and requires licensing for most uses. DBpedia, the Linked Open Data knowledge base that pulls and publishes data from Wikipedia, is, on the other hand, open and can be freely used, modified, and shared by anyone for any purpose.

Again, HOW it works is less important to us than why it works, much the same way that the nuances of Latin syntax or verb conjugation matter less than the greater fact that everyone communicating in Latin from the Roman Empire through at least the 19th century was working in the same knowledge space.

What can *you* do to help your library prepare? Number one on the list is: Educate yourself further and become an advocate for Linked Open Data at your library. When opportunities appear for having your catalog published as Linked Open Data, you want your leadership or administrative team to already know that it's a good idea worth investing in.

Second, be extraordinarily scrupulous with your oral history metadata. It is more than likely hyper-local, and when your library publishes its records as Linked Open Data, your URIs can be unique in the world. Which means if you don't get the names, surnames, dates of birth/death, localities, and/or event names correct, there is no other authority to defer to, and that can have far-reaching consequences. Your records will be cited—whether by a genealogist, historian, or general researcher—and your records will have the weight of the library's authority behind them. Make sure they are as correct as they can be.

Elsewhere in this text is mentioned saving your oral history metadata somewhere separate from your MARC records. This is a good idea. Not to say that your catalogers are remiss in their duties; however, some information, in translation, can end up on the floor. If you maintain your metadata in a standard format, such as Qualified Dublin Core or Metadata Object Description Schema (MODS), preferably in a system that can export to XML (Extensible Markup Language) (which just makes things that much more convenient), then you will be well-positioned to have your metadata transformed and published alongside or with your library's MARC records.

Adam Spiers

Attending a conference, I heard an interview excerpt in which a gentleman described being caught in a hurricane—specifically, caught in a tree in a hurricane—with winds so powerful that first his clothes were blown off and then his dentures ripped from his mouth. Estimating that there was a good chance he would die, the man's response was: "Well, I came into the world naked and without teeth; I may as well leave that way." This story remains lodged in my memory because (a) it shows human resiliency and amazing capacity for humor and (b) it illustrates the power of oral history to add meaning to data and to deliver information. Coming from Colorado, I may read about a hurricane and see a data point like "winds of 100 mph"—but I have no reference, no connection to that number as it relates to wind. When I hear someone vividly and creatively describe the physical experience of being in that hurricane, my brain can quantify the impact, and a switch is turned.

Whatever the opportunity, oral history needs to be placed within the retrieval systems most likely to garner an audience. How can you participate in the Semantic Web? How can you become part of the linked data movement? How can you organize and represent your content to take advantage of the most elegant and efficient advancements? Librarians directly working with oral history are positioned to apply these evolving search utilities, publishing metadata to expose new connections to community voice. The idea of shifting business practices for every book already cataloged in a library system is daunting, but small-scale collections of wholly unique content (a.k.a., oral history) are ripe for experimentation. The Internet can become a place where people don't just bump into "things" but encounter *meaning*.

FINISHING THOUGHTS

Writing this chapter has been challenging—blending concrete suggestions with concepts just out of explanatory reach. At the time when you are reading this (if this book has a long shelf life), the application of the Semantic Web might be well underway, and perhaps you are laughing at my novice attempts to touch on "future" possibilities. I hope this is true, and I hope that firsthand testimony has been made prevalent in and pertinent to our frameworks for examining the world. However, if the hoped-for scenario has yet to be realized, I implore you to solve the problem—or be part of the solution. Contribute your thinking to a metadata standard for oral history; bone up on FRBR and RDF; educate yourself about ontologies and help create one for oral history. And if the preceding ideas are too much, simply ensure that your library catalog has full surrogate records for every interview in your collection.

A distant way of thinking about resource organization relied on "classification," where a theoretical slot existed for each unique manifestation of knowledge. But oral history eschews classification; the nature of the material is too complicated. Instead, oral history must be organized through relationships. The actions you take toward representing the content of interviews will help or hinder connection to an outside audience. And connection is the goal, making possible the transfer of idea, experience, and impact.

NOTES

1. Arlene G. Taylor and Daniel N. Joudrey, *The Organization of Information*. 3rd ed. (Westport, CT: Libraries Unlimited, 2009).

2. *Merriam-Webster's* (2003). The range of definitions cover media formats from voice to instrument to DNA (genetic coding). Interesting to think of transcription, broadly, as a transferal.

3. With digital files, you find a huge variety of platforms for delivering recordings. And the advance of playback technologies leaves no excuse for *not* making recordings available to the public, without specific reason for restriction.

4. An example of speech-to-text service was Pop Up Archive. (Closed for business from November 2017.)

5. Express Scribe is a software freely available for download; Transcribe is a web application that works with Google Chrome and has some excellent features, though costing $20 per year.

6. A researcher studying linguistics may have specific interest in seeing fillers, which may be representative of social trends or patterns.

7. My presentation of FRBR is based mostly on the discussions integrated into Arlene Taylor's *Understanding FRBR: What It Is and How It Will Affect Our Retrieval Tools*. Someday, perhaps, in a new manifestation of that text, a chapter will be added for "FRBR and Oral History: Mapping Out a Metadata Standard."

8. The national Oral History Association started organizing a Metadata Task Force in 2014. A roundtable presentation was given during the 2017 OHA conference in Minneapolis, MN. "Surveying the Field: An OHA Metadata Task Force Roundtable."

9. Arlene G. Taylor and Daniel N. Joudrey, *The Organization of Information*. 3rd ed. (Westport, CT: Libraries Unlimited, 2009).

10. Variously referred to as the "wisdom hierarchy," or DIKW, Ackoff's model saw its earliest formal presentation in 1989, in the *Journal of Applied Systems Analysis*.

4

Reach = Dissemination

Chapter Three covered steps critical to the progress of the long-term goal: transforming individual story into shared knowledge. If the challenge of organizing and representing oral history content seems amorphous, let your spirits be lifted—this chapter is about the satisfaction of putting oral history into the memory of the community. The field has been plotted, the soil turned and tilled, the rows carved out ... and now you get to drop the seeds. With objects such as books or DVDs, traditional library service includes strategies for shifting materials to spots where patrons can make a pick-up. Shifting—or sharing—oral history is a different endeavor and easier in some ways, because you aren't required to track the interview as a physical object. Also, you aren't required to place limits on the time an interview rests in the possession of any one person or the community on whole. With oral history, your options include everybody having access to the same oral histories, at any time desired, for as long as the desire to listen exists.

DELIVERING CONTENT

The action of placing oral history into the reach of the community is something of a culminating event. At the same time, the plan for how this happens cannot occur after the content has been brought into existence—it cannot be an afterthought. This book's title refers to "Shelf Space for Voice," which is a clarion metaphor. For voice to occupy a place in your library, first your mind must be opened to the relevance of personal experience; you

> The plan for how this happens cannot occur after the content has been brought into existence—it cannot be an afterthought.

must carve out time and energy to facilitate the oral history process; and you must commit to a system of delivery, where the public is invited to receive the oral history item (of the *manifestation* of the *expression* of the *work*). The select vehicle for bringing oral history to the community must accommodate your purpose, and it must be suited for the job.

Before exploring the "transportation" options, a quick note about the object of delivery: Oral history is at its best when you find an audience absorbed by the words being spoken, the stories being shared. So, remember that *what* you are delivering is *voice*. Your job is to establish a platform—or tiers of platforms—to support the aural transmission of firsthand experience; the delivery of speech is the high mark of your aim. Also, the recipients of the interview must be kept in mind. Who is the community you intend to reach with your oral histories? Think beyond those who have been interviewed or those in your geographic proximity. The body of people who can learn from your work is expansive; the stories in your collection, no doubt, hit themes that will find resonance in disparate locations. Showing imagination for who you might touch is central to the act of preparing your delivery.

Virtual Portals

In the context of this book, *virtual* is understood as "existing online." At the same time, the connotation of "near enough" is worth observing. Some learning opportunities demand proximity to an original artifact—the Sistine Chapel or the Great Pyramid of Giza—and oral history is not one of those instances. You can be sitting in your living room, connected to the Internet, listening to an interview with a Chernobyl survivor, and be utterly transported. The Latin root of virtual is *virtus*, meaning strength, and the Internet's strong virtue is prominent with the delivery of oral history content. The opportunity to listen from a distance means that you can be in a location most comfortable for your physical needs and suitable for your attention to the interview. Or, you can be at the site of an event dramatized in an interview and bring the narrator's words—literally—with you. The merging of place and voice is possible through a networked environment.

Advanced and specialized skills such as web design and construction are beyond the purview of this book. However, know that you can establish a web presence, an oral history site, with relative ease. For your library to disseminate interview content, some type of publishing platform must be selected. Open-source and low-cost (or free) examples include WordPress or Omeka.[1] But before examining platforms, you need to have in mind the characteristics that make a virtual experience effective for any digital item and especially for oral history. And, you must anticipate the growth of your work, your ambitions, and your product. Unless your goals are static, the platform you select must accommodate delivery of oral history materials into the foreseeable future. Think about continuity and predictability.

Storage

Your aim is to let people check out, or sample, interview content online, just as they would if picking up a book at the library—so you'll need space for storing all electronic files that you intend to share. Interview excerpts can be excellent for hooking people's interest, but they are no substitute for the full package. Chapter Two (Record) addressed the pros and cons of audio and video capture for oral history. One hefty concern for video is the comparatively large—exponentially greater—file size. A price will be paid if you expect to place those video interviews into the virtual reach of the public.

You have the choice of overseeing server administration (locally hosted) or paying some dollar amount to place that responsibility with an outside provider. Either option might be most suitable for your library—the decision is steered by local know-how, support, and server capacity; your anticipation for collection growth; monetary resources; and available time for administering updates, tweaks, or upgrades. Audio files can be compressed to free up storage space without compromising much, if anything, in the way of listenability. Remember that human conversation is not comparable to instrumental recordings, in terms of the desired end product and the impetus for creating the recording in the first place. With oral history, the goal is to clearly understand what is being spoken and expressed—and you can deliver that outcome even with a compressed audio file.

A sensible approach to web dissemination is to start with a defined project, weighing the options for storage and *every* considered aspect. If you have a large collection of oral histories, create a sampler and use that subset to explore decisions. You will see how much space is required for interviews and other complementary objects such as transcripts and photo images. By far, the most demanding storage component of your web presence will be the interview content, and you can predictably upscale the requirements before making extra monetary investments.

Display and Search

The KISS principle of simplicity (keep it simple . . .) is a potent design edict, particularly when you want users to experience the oral history and not a cacophony of distractions. One thing that must be completely obvious to users is the "play" function of the interview, most recognizable by the right-facing triangle. After a person lands at the website, and by whatever means he or she arrived (more on this later), each oral history record must be presented as a distinct object that can be played. The central purpose for creating the site is the conveyance of oral history; do not bury the opportunity to listen. To that end, draft what you'd hope to see, once an oral history is located:

- Title for the interview (e.g., "Oral History Interview with Smeetluft Jambor")
- A "play" window for audio or video

- Metadata for that interview
- Transcript for that interview (if it exists)
- Index or summary for that interview (if it exists)
- Photo images associated with that interview (if they exist)

All of the elements that advance the comprehension of the oral history should be bundled into a single-page view. Make sure you have a one-to-one relationship between what you are showing and what you are providing.[2] This means that any displayed information (metadata) must pertain to what is available online, unless explicitly directed otherwise (e.g., "The Carnegie Library has file folders with clippings related to this interview.") When audio is not available for a given oral history (maybe the file has been lost or has not been loaded), do not suggest the presence of sound with a title such as "Audio Recording of Smeetluft Jambor." This would confuse and frustrate members of the public who then anticipate the opportunity to listen. Instead, have a more generic/truthful title such as "Oral History Interview," which can have different manifestations.

The publishing platform you choose will have a dashboard that organizes your placement of metadata and descriptive content. If you made the effort to draft abstracts and list keywords and topics associated with interviews, be sure these pointers are situated in searchable fields. You want users to locate interviews based on what is discussed, not just who is doing the talking; you want the public to explore the oral histories and uncover content beyond what they expected before coming to the website. Platforms have different options for search configurations—from simple to advanced—allowing Boolean combinations, exact-match limiters, and facet filters. Depending on the quantity of interviews in your collection, you may do well to stick with a basic search, which is likely to bring up the most results. Test the search feature on at least one planted interview and *then* make decisions about how to tweak the settings. Read the documentation about the platform's features, so you can anticipate what is being probed for match results—and make sure your site's indexing is up to date. Finally, make the search box prominent and appealing, with a title that indicates what is being explored (e.g., "Search the Oral History Collection").

Functionality

The previous chapter made the case for transcribing interviews—including time stamps—and at least summarizing or indexing the content. The utility of these efforts is fully shown with the simultaneous presentation of a play function for audio/video plus a typed transcript/index. Hopefully, the recording quality of the audio is high, but if that's not the case, a transcript can help make the content clear. A user can be listening to the interview and following along with the transcript. Also, and much more common: With the simultaneous display of document and sound, researchers can scan the transcript for portions most relevant to their specific interest, and then immediately navigate to those spots of the recorded interview—this accomplished without shifting between web pages. Ideally, the presentation of the transcript/summary will also have a full-text searching option, akin to the "find" function associated with Word documents. If a researcher is looking for the mention of a particular name, that word can be located throughout the interview, correlated with points in the conversation.

One application for enhancing the accessibility of the recorded interview/transcript/index is called Oral History Metadata Synchronizer (OHMS).[3] Using this application, your transcript or index can be synchronized with the original recording. Then, a researcher would not need to manually navigate to specific portions of the original recording; time stamps would be synched with the audio, and clicking the stamp on the web-displayed transcript would take you to that moment in the interview. The same thing could happen for words in the transcript—or, in the case of an OHMS-doctored index, a user could be jumped to summarized portions of the interview. OHMS is available for free and open-source distribution, so the investment on your part would be one of extra time in learning and configuring the system, and then further processing your materials to utilize the technology.

> Are you meeting the needs of the public who will be interacting with your interviews?

As you weigh options about how to improve (hopefully) the functionality of your web presence, consider one question: Are you meeting the needs of the public who will be interacting with your interviews? Are you assisting their engagement with the oral histories? The sole purpose for having a site is the dissemination of content—that is, putting interviews into the reach of the community. Ask yourself, what is minimally required for making the interviews functional? If you have a transcript that includes time stamps every minute or two, and you have a play window that allows a user to move the play bar to different points in the interview, you are meeting a minimum threshold. With more time processing, and more embellishments to your website, will you be increasing public engagement? Is there a chance that the efforts create more complexity than is helpful to your specific audience?

Use

Once you establish a website presence, you will want evidence that it is being explored, as well as data on how people are interacting with the oral histories. The "how" is a reflection of functionality, where you learn about peoples' interests and preferences, balanced with the terms and conditions for utilizing interviews. Naturally, in delivering interviews back to the community, the hope is that content will be applied toward something. When people hear the interviews, their understanding is informed by what is being spoken. And that is an immediate and worthy outcome. At the same time, new forms of information should come from the oral histories—books, art, exhibits, and programs—where the content assists in creating further education and interpretation. This extension is the greater goal, and it is achieved by permitting the public to manipulate the original recordings.

Be sure to post a rights statement and explanation of what is allowed and/ or required in order for interviews to be repurposed—the conditions to be met for content to be extended. Chapter Two covers the release form that is jointly signed by the narrator and the interviewer. That form also makes note of what might happen with interviews; be sure that both notations have the same intent and similar, if not identical, wording. A source that might be helpful with wording is the Creative Commons community (https:// creativecommons.org/), which provides the language and legal terms for several copyright licenses. Creative Commons emphasizes knowledge sharing, and it is designed for Internet content and use. The Commons site is practical, offering comprehensible explanations in addition to legal wording and icons that depict selected licenses. In spirit, the Commons is philosophical, encouraging "universal access to research and education, full participation in culture."

Many oral history websites allow the download of PDF versions of transcripts; some online repositories also allow audio files to be downloaded; still other collections instruct that people who want to acquire their own copy of any part of the interview must contact the organization. And, at least one library—Houston Public—requires that the public agree to a disclaimer before even listening online.[4] Weighing the options, here are things to consider:

- Regardless of what is specified in your "terms of use" statement, making files downloadable expedites the chance that they will be used for an external purpose that may or may not agree with your intentions.
- Do you want to know about how interview content is being used? Do you want to preapprove external uses?
- If you require that the public request interview content, is there a form to be submitted? And what is your plan for delivering the requested audio/video/transcript? Will there be a fee associated?
- If *only* the transcript is available for download, expect that it will get used as the "primary" document, supplanting the original recording in that role.
- What does your community anticipate from the library? Are your actions in accordance with community needs and expectations?

Of course, the question of how to respond depends on the premise that people have arrived at the website in the first place. In MARC records, you can use the 856 tag to embed URLs for associated interviews. Patrons who use the library catalog and discover the oral histories will thereby have a quick link to the online recordings—made possible by the interview having its own page on the website where it resides. Routing people through the library for access is helpful in establishing the source connection, and it might be the first way that anyone learns about your website. From this initial exposure, users can bookmark the web address and directly navigate there to explore additional interview content.

Lastly, in considering a publishing platform, be aware of the options for tracking site visits and page views, which correlates to interview interaction; make sure you have the ability to harness a tool like Google Analytics. More nuanced data might include the number of minutes users spend with any one interview, or usage of specific collections, or geographic locations for site users. Quantitative data behind the public's interaction will be important for demonstrating the value of time spent creating and maintaining the website. Numbers can be included in reports and presentations—and pitches for more dollars to fund the oral history activities!

Physical/Tactile Portals

Returning Interviews to Narrators

An integral part of oral history is connecting with the narrator: making sure that he or she feels gratified by the experience; communicating the library's appreciation for the individual contribution; and making clear that his or her story is being valued for its power to inform. Placing the interview within the library holdings is one way of showing this respect. In addition, gifting the recording of the interview back to the narrator is both thoughtful and ethical. You want the person to understand that by participating in an oral history, he or she has not given anything away; rather, the narrator has acquired a tangible expression of his experience—it has been made real and accessible to others.

Options for returning the interview to the narrator, via physical media, continually evolve. Whereas cassette tapes used to be common for making duplicates, now the recording file can be burned or saved to CD or DVD or placed onto a flash drive and mailed or delivered in person. The plus side to providing a physical object is composite: First, the narrator literally feels as though he or she is receiving something—a nice reinforcement of the equal exchange between library and individual. Also, the library has an opportunity to brand itself on the media that is offered back: a screen print or label on the CD/DVD, or a branded flash drive. Presuming that family will think of the oral history as a keepsake and want to preserve the recording, this can be something that gets passed on between generations, and the library's presence becomes embedded in the family. The downside is that the medium will likely *only* be a reminder of the oral history experience, a physical token versus something functional for preserving/playing the interview. Optical media (CD/DVD) once thought to be enduring is now shown to be unpredictable in life span—not to mention that a scratch can render the disc unplayable. But then, how long will CD/DVD drives exist? Already they are being phased out of laptops and work stations. So if a CD/DVD is used as the means for returning the recording, it should be formatted like a USB, so the discrete interview files can be pulled off, copied, and saved to the family's preferred electronic storage (remember LOCKSS).

A third option for sharing back the interview is via a cloud-host service, like Dropbox, Box, Google Drive, or OneDrive. Files can be placed in these

storage sites for an amount of time, allowing the narrator or family to download. A service like TransferBigFiles might suffice for uploading a file and then emailing a link that is temporarily available. Before making any hard-and-fast decisions about media and delivery formats, speak with the narrator and allow that person—and that person's family—to state a preference; make sure the narrator is comfortable with the delivery mechanism. And lastly, if you won't be using physical media to return the original recording, consider making some other material keepsake as evidence of the oral history.[5] Imagine a future generation that is not aware of the interview having taken place, discovering a certificate of appreciation and then contacting the library. When, at that time, you are able to give the voice of a loved one back to the family, you will find no greater satisfaction.

Library Checkout

And lastly, if your library lists CDs and DVDs for checkout, why not include oral history? Once you start gathering collections of interviews and gaining repute for the quality of the product, you may discover that people want to take home a CD, DVD, or flash drive that contains an oral history. These patrons have no intent to repurpose the interview but might simply want to listen to the recording in the privacy of their own space, or plan a gathering and create a shared experience—it could be for a family gathering, book group, or other social function. Interviews can be burned onto a single CD or DVD—formatted for CD/DVD player—and then placed in a jewel case. Or, with a flash drive, you could store many requested files and then wipe and reuse the drive for different patrons. When planning to circulate oral history recordings, consider the following:

- What is the community level of interest? Are circulation requests so infrequent that systematizing a response would be a waste of time?
- If you are operating as a stand-alone branch or other solo setting, do you need to use the patron services component of your ILS for this distribution function? Or, is the demand infrequent enough that you can track items using a spreadsheet and a calendar?
- Are you using the patron's library card to monitor the checkout/return of the physical medium? If not using a library card for tracking, what exchange will be required?

Library Listening Stations

With oral history recordings, many narrators want to make their voices part of the library collection but don't want their oral histories distributed online. For those instances, you must accommodate in-library listening. Even on the chance that every oral history participant has consented to web distribution, some community members might need or enjoy coming to the library and interacting with interviews while on the premises. This would be a good opportunity for you to explain the goals of the library's oral history activities.

Staging a listening station shouldn't be complicated or costly—earphones might be the only outright purchase. If the library already has a bank of computer stations, one computer can be designated as the oral history terminal; on that machine, create an electronic folder that contains all interview files, and make the oral history website the default home page. Having visitors use the website from within the library could be advantageous; it would allow you to observe how people respond to the features—what makes a positive impression or what causes confusion. As an alternative to a full workstation, many libraries keep at least one laptop, netbook, or Chromebook available for patron use. One of these options can work for playing interviews that are not available for web sharing but have been loaded to a flash drive. If you are finding that very few people want or need to play oral recordings at the library, you might stipulate that visitors communicate their desire in advance, allowing time for the preparation of a computer/laptop as well as interview files.

Folders with Supplemental Content

If your library is prepared to go somewhat further, you might establish an oral history shelf that contains a single folder (at minimum) for every interview in the collection. This serves as a place to put transcript pages as well as any other print material that supports the content of the interview. Through the course of conducting oral histories, you may find that narrators are eager to share documents that explain, illustrate, or validate the experiences about which they speak: business papers, clipped articles, brochures, and flyers. The supplemental documents simply might demonstrate personality— letters, artwork, or photographs. A photocopy or scan of the original material would be fine, as the purpose is not to show "originality" but to provide greater information, to add depth and context to the topics of the recorded interview. These folders would not need to be organized and described in the way of finding aids that exist for archival holdings. Keep it simple. A field note (e.g., 599 tag in MARC) or other indicator in the catalog record could alert the public to the possibility of complementary paper documents, and this might encourage other members of the community to donate additional information where it exists.

SUPPLEMENTAL MATERIALS

In this chapter, you learn that collecting materials is supplemental to the interview, but let's take a closer look at that topic. At my library, we had quite a bit of supplemental materials in our collections, and actively sought them out.

There are two issues to reflect on when considering this path for your collections:

1. Space limitations
2. Potential use

If you are just starting to build a local history collection, oral history is a great vehicle for bringing other "things" into the library and can offer a great proof of concept for funding. If you can get a few square feet of floor space, a filing cabinet is a great start to a collection of supplementary materials. You just need to alert your donors as to the level of security you have available. A file cabinet open to the public is perfectly acceptable so long as the materials are replaceable copies. Anything more valuable (original World War II V-Cards for instance) should be held under a higher level of security than some institutions may be willing to support at first. Some level of staff supervision of unique materials is always warranted, including retrieval from a secured space (locked file cabinet or room), providing any necessary instruction and overseeing use, and returning items, all of which take time away from other duties. Programs do grow and develop out into vaults and reading rooms with specialized staff and security apparatus when value is demonstrated though!

If you are looking to provide access to additional information, and are not so interested in intrinsic or artifactual value, scanning materials and making them available online will keep your physical footprint small and may even increase the quality of materials donated. Many interviewees, while very interested in adding to the collective knowledge on a subject, are loath to part with personal materials that hold significant intrinsic emotional value. Better to provide access to a scanned letter than no letter at all.

However, when the door opens to supplemental materials, you can easily find yourself in the position of having more offered than you or your patrons can utilize. You might hear something like this: "Oh! If you want photos, I have *albums full* that you can have!" Beware this reality: Sometimes someone's personal collection is valuable only to them, and the library may appear to be a fantastic repository in lieu of interested family. Don't create an arbitrary policy to lean on in such situations. Rather, make sure you give thought to what you can responsibly maintain and express that to the donor. This is about stewardship, and it is perfectly reasonable to ask for only the best and most rewarding materials on behalf of your patrons.

The best materials to acquire are those that support the narrative of the interview in ways that the interview cannot. Pictures and maps fall easily into this category with their ability to rapidly convey spatial relationships, context, and other visual information. Reports, journals, letters, and related publications can go into much more specific detail on a subject than might be warranted in the interview itself. For instance, a ship's log will be much more specific and exhaustive than nearly anyone on the ship could be in relating exact times and locations.

Above all else, make sure that you are going to be able to make these resources available somehow. I have seen photocopies in slim three-ring binders on the shelf, and I have likewise seen vaults built to house originals. I have also seen collections end up in boxes on shelves with no metadata and no representation in the general catalog. They might as well not exist at that point—a situation which, left unresolved, will inevitably tarnish your reputation. Whatever your resources available, get the information out in any way you responsibly can, and build from there. There is nothing wrong with starting small, only with not getting started.

Adam Spiers

BUILDING BRIDGES TO THE COMMUNITY

The first section of this chapter focused on dissemination, considering the ways a library can facilitate content delivery to the community. But equally important, when thinking about "reach," is the contact between library and community, where exchange of ideas takes place, utilizing the stories from within oral history. This is the exciting juncture at which new growth occurs—when the prophecy of oral history is fulfilled. This happens only when the public actually experiences the interviews from your collection.

Explanation and Promotion

When you have put time and energy into establishing a place for oral history in your library, you want people to know about it. A simple fact about messaging: You must thoroughly understand what you are explaining, why it is important, and to whom it will have relevance. Chapter One addresses collection development from the standpoint of recognition—being keen to what is needed by the community that can be provided by the library through oral history. With that in mind, *know* and be able to *show* the reason for the library's engagement with oral history. List the goals and objectives that are fulfilled through pursuing oral history; make clear the positive impact that will result from the library's commitment to documenting primary knowledge.

With oral history, you have a first line of messengers in the people who participate in the interviews—those who are conducting the oral history on behalf of the library, and the narrators who will speak with others about the interview experience. These individuals must enter into and come away from the oral history with an understanding of what is being accomplished. Do not assume that interviewees are familiar with the practice of oral history—provide them with a description of the discipline, what it entails, and how it compares to journalism or storytelling. Have a prepared statement about the role of oral history in building the library's collection and identity, and its service to community. This should be conveyed, in part, on the consent/release form that is signed by interview participants, but you might have something more tailored and inspirational to give to narrators. Something like this:

> Oral history is the process of recording first-hand experiences. The conversation involves an interviewer and a narrator, who is selected for his/her depth of knowledge in a subject area. The interview may focus on the narrator's life experience or his/her account of a specified topic, event, place, or time. Oral history is original information; interviews are raw material that can be used to create new kinds of documentation or experiential information (e.g. books, films, exhibits). Oral history is one way the library fulfills its mission of helping people engage with information that can enrich their lives.

And then, be sure that interviewers are prepared to speak on the merits of oral history and its function in the library. The people who you speak with are the ambassadors for the library's oral history activities. To the extent that any one person is willing, make sure that every person feels a pull to encourage participation from the community.

A second line of messaging is your library or consortium website, where visitors can discover information about baseline objectives, projects, and practices. This also would be a place to invite more participation and expand the opportunities for involvement, empowering the community to suggest ideas for new interviews and subjects to explore. Promotion is not *just* about pushing something that already has been done; to properly promote a collection, you should honor, advance, and further the development of source material. Use the library website, the oral history website, or any other platform to draw in more contributions. Grow your anticipation for what is possible. And remember, if you have concretely explained the parameters of focus, means, and outcome, you will receive suggestions that are aligned with development values.

Lastly, tap into other ways that community receives information: local newspapers, newsletters, radio, or television. How can those outlets pitch the collection? Do people get email updates from organizations and/or businesses? (Or the city, or the library?) What listservs are utilized and by whom? Think about *different* audiences you want to reach—not just individuals who are library members, but outside agents who might be in a position to support your activities through donations or word-of-mouth praise. What are the kindred organizations—cultural heritage, arts, and theater—that could assist with cross-promotion? To the extent that you want people to know about what is happening with oral history, pursue all appropriate avenues, be consistent with your messaging, and prepare an "elevator speech."

Programming

Once you have a body of interviews, the possibilities for reflection and discovery start to materialize. A larger quantity of voices provides greater territory for exploration—but even a few oral histories are groundwork on which to build programming.

Engaging with the Content

Whatever the subject matter of an interview—whether narrowly focused or wide-ranging in touch points—oral history gives you the reason and the substance to create dialogue in the community. In Chapter Three, you learned of the importance of establishing access points to a recording: transcript, abstract, keyword and topic lists. That initial time investment pays off when you want to return to the recording over the years. You can't predict what portion of the full interview will offer illumination at a future date, but knowing what it holds, you will be able to mine the resource as occasions for programming emerge.

Here are two ways to think about utilizing interview content: "outside looking in" and "inside looking out." *Outside looking in* means that something is transpiring in the community, and you should pull together content that responds to the event. The impetus could come from infinite sources: joyous, tragic, historic, artistic, environmental ... small or monumental. Anything happening in the community might cause you to explore interviews for relevant content. For example, during a seasonal holiday, you might plan an event where community brings objects, food, and stories pertinent to their own traditions; during that event, play clips from interviews, illustrating past seasonal traditions. Or maybe you are planning an author talk, and the subject of the book can be made more relevant by listening to oral histories of associated content; or maybe the author is someone from the community, and you have an oral history with that individual's mother—imagine the poignancy of an author introduction that incorporates the mother's voice. (Check first with the author!) If you are part of a library system with multiple branches, discover what programs are being planned and insert oral history into the mix, where it fits.

Inside looking out means that you recognize content from one or more interviews that needs to be reintroduced to the community. Oral history is often strategic for gathering perspectives that have been neglected in other forms of documentation (perhaps an interview in your collection is the only primary evidence of Olympic accomplishments from a local athlete). As you discover content that is novel, or malnourished in the psyche of the community, build discussion around those topics. Every time you have an "aha" moment from hearing something in an interview, think about whether that moment can be amplified at a community level through programming.

> The most potent use for oral history *is* the topic of perplexing difficulty, where data points are not sufficient as evidence, and no single perspective sums up the feelings and emotions.

Finally: Do not shy away from difficult topics. The most potent use for oral history *is* the topic of perplexing difficulty, where data points are not sufficient as evidence, and no single perspective sums up the feelings and emotions. If something complex is challenging your community—be it social, political, or economic—plan an event that introduces that topic through recorded interviews. This way, attendees are less tempted to interrupt or shout down the opinions of others—it is a way of showing multiple perspectives that are at odds, without putting *people* at odds.

Engaging with the Format

A program focusing on content from oral history—as previously discussed—would involve the playing of sound, video, or blended media (combination of sound, video, and/or still photos). Instruction on how to create these play options could be another type of programming. What makes a good soundtrack for voice? What are you listening for? What are the options for audio and video editing? What are the techniques? How do you create a compact "story" from a full oral history? How do you create a mini-documentary (think of Ken Burns) involving a combination of oral history, photographs, and music? Digging into these questions might comprise a series of workshops facilitated by people in the community with expertise: radio production, video production, and digital storytelling. And this might be the kind of programming that draws people of different age groups, as younger folks have greater ease or curiosity about production tools.

Lastly: A follow-up to instructional programming would be a show-and-tell, where people demonstrate techniques learned and discuss results.

Engaging with the People

Often with oral history, a person will finish the interview and then realize he or she has so much more to tell. The completion of a lengthy recording soon is met by a desire to say more or to think more about whatever topic or topics were attended to during the conversation. Your library can create this opportunity—create programming around the people whose stories are part of your collection. If you have a set of interviews focused on a subject, where people with different experiences explain their involvement or their understanding, invite those people to participate in a panel discussion. You might play excerpts from interviews and allow people to reflect on their words and sentiments, in comparison with others. Or maybe you have a "Talk Again" program, where people who have been interviewed get the chance to speak on that experience.

An idea dating back to 2000 but gaining some traction recently is the *Human Library*.[6] This programming format encourages conversations with people from groups that may have been stigmatized or not even recognized. Volunteers apply a "title" to themselves—Alcoholic, Brain Damaged, Fat Woman, or Polyamorous—and then place themselves on loan for "checkout." Library visitors can select titles and then listen to the experiences of that person through the lens of whatever label they've chosen. The idea is to bridge divides and connect individuals who may never have spoken or would not have talked honestly about their stigmas. Also, it's a way of seeing more diversity in a community, beyond obvious traits, appearances, or categories. From an existing oral history collection, you may find people to participate in this type of program at your library. Or maybe a Human Library format becomes the basis for an oral history collection, where individuals are recorded and then their titles are made part of the library.

Remember, the narrator is not the only participant in an oral history recording. The interviewer plays an integral role and that person can be tapped to contribute to programming. The work of being an interviewer involves preparation and execution; an explanation of that work might be useful for a library presentation, focusing on research skills, listening techniques, or "the art of oral history." Time spent in active listening—which is the goal for oral history—has a lasting impact, and the story of the interviewer might be one that the community needs to hear.

Bringing Together Content, Format, and People

StoryCenter (formerly the Center for Digital Storytelling) started in 1993 as an organization dedicated to story facilitation—putting people in touch with what they want to say—and digital media production, as a method for encapsulating a story message. StoryCenter hosts public workshops that teach skills and techniques; they also work with communities on initiatives to address topics of concern, using the digital storytelling model.

StoryCenter has a history of working with libraries, and their shop might be a starter kit for programming.[7]

During a StoryCenter workshop, people write and then record themselves reading their reflections. This recording, then, is the basis for layers of image and sound that shapes a brief (2–4 minutes) video message. This blending of intent, method, and personality can be exercised with oral history collections. Within a full oral history—which may be an hour-long recording—individual portions offer compelling narrative, in the same way that a constructed story commands attention. Library programming might involve having narrators listen to their own oral histories, to identify the places where they hear a particular truth emerge. Original excerpts can be the basis for a digital story production—or, the recognition of those parts might encourage a narrator to draft something more intentional to be read and recorded. The exercise of mining "story" from oral history also could be a community or classroom workshop, creating a body of digital stories that are shown to narrators (or family) during a special program.

Presentations and (Social) Media

Programming involves planned interactions for learning, taking place at the library. But the community also can be reached via presentations or media posts. Look for opportunities to speak to public or private organizations: historical or genealogical societies, educational institutions, and religious or social groups for all ages. Don't rely on bringing people to the library; go to where the people are, and talk about what you are doing or planning for oral history. Visit classrooms and encourage oral history to be integrated into curriculum.[8] Think about designated "awareness" months (black history, women's history, and poetry) and how you might represent any particular theme. Your job is not to tell people how to feel about any given topic, but you can explain how people *are* feeling by exposing oral history content that relates to themes.

Social media like Facebook, Instagram, Pinterest, or Snapchat are great venues for messaging about oral history projects or happenings. Just remember that these outlets get oxygen from regular posting, so before diving in, evaluate whether you'll be able to keep up and if you have enough "news" to push with regularity. On the other hand, local radio can become a partner for less frequent broadcasts that are coordinated in advance and can be highly produced. These might coincide with events and programming taking place at

> Your job is not to tell people how to feel about any given topic, but you can explain how people *are* feeling by exposing oral history content that relates to themes.

the library—or they might become the impetus for further programming, if public response is positive.

FINISHING THOUGHTS

For an oral history to be maximally accessible, it needs to be discoverable, understandable, and available—and it must exist in a format that people can and will use. This chapter on "Reach" combines all of these elements to show that an integrated approach is necessary, and it can be accomplished through a variety of means within *your* reach. Exploring practical channels for disseminating content, what must not be lost is the more abstract concept of touch: making sure your work touches the community, and allowing that same experience for yourself. To conclude, I will again turn to the poignant reflections of Denver Public Library's Jim Kroll:

CN: **What was it like when you had the exhibit here?**

JK: Well, they came to see it. And it was wonderful. We had an open house one Saturday morning, to celebrate, and the neighborhood came. Families, children, elderly people; people from all different ethnic communities that were represented there. And they came. . . .

CN: **What, if any, relations do you now have with the community?**

JK: Of course, afterwards, the whole I-70 proposal became a major issue—not only for the neighborhoods, but for the city and county of Denver. There were people who were passionately opposed to the proposal that CDOT and the federal government came up with. Oh! Well, that makes it an interesting—there's an interesting part to that. Because of that controversy, students as well as individuals from the community came in to find out what we have, and that's how they discovered some of the oral histories. . . .

CN: **How does the outcome that you see now, with the project—how does that compare with what your imagination was for the project?**

JK: Hmmm. Well, as a good librarian, I was just thinking that, you know, we would collect the histories of the neighborhood—especially the oral histories and interviews with the residents. Then you put it on the shelf, and you catalog it, and it's there. And you move on to the next thing. But, to see how these three neighborhoods have been such a big part of the news in recent years means that this collection was beginning to have life in ways unanticipated. . . .

I keep a photograph from that exhibit in my office. It's the one up there, with a gentleman who is mowing his lawn, and a very friendly dog at the fence. The house is very simple; it's just a wood-framed house, with a front porch. But the yard is well maintained; there is obviously great pride that goes on by the owner, as to how his property—he's presenting his property to the rest of the neighborhood. That's very true of those three neighborhoods. What I found, through Judy's eyes, was a definite love for its residents and its history.

NOTES

1. For open-source web publishing platforms, user forums and meetups will provide more support and advice than you could ever hope to absorb.

2. The Dublin Core Metadata Initiative (DCMI) talks about the "one-to-one principle" in associating a given resource with its given description. This ties into a Linked Data environment, when unique identifiers can be assigned to every instantiation of original artifacts, such as prints of the Mona Lisa (or a Mona Lisa postcard, poster, cartoon, etc.).

3. Doug Boyd, "OHMS: Enhancing Access to Oral History for Free," The Oral History Review, January 1, 2013, vol. 40, no. 1, pp. 95–106. https://doi.org/10.1093/ohr/oht031.

4. The Houston Oral History Project (http://www.houstonoralhistory.org/) includes a variety of interview collections that stem from different source points: commissioned oral histories, digitized oral histories, and special projects. Most are made available through the Houston Public Library Digital Archives: http://digital.houstonlibrary.org/.

5. The idea of making a fancy letter or certificate was put forward by a volunteer for the Maria Rogers Oral History Program. At a meeting, the volunteer group discussed the quandary of how to accommodate changing media formats and delivery options, while remaining considerate of family wishes—and thinking about what would be important into the future.

6. The Human Library is a framework for conversations. Their site explains the idea, origin, and ongoing activity: http://humanlibrary.org/.

7. StoryCenter, formerly Center for Digital Storytelling: https://www.storycenter.org/. StoryCenter started marketing "Listening Stations" in conjunction with what the organization describes as "re-inventing oral history."

8. The national Oral History Association has a resource section dedicated to educators: http://www.oralhistory.org/educators-resource/.

5

Reflect

In previous chapters, you learned how a person's individual experience joins a communal body of knowledge when oral history is brought into existence and stewarded by the library. Each of the four stages—cast as four Rs in this text—involves specific activities grounded in foundational library practices: Collection Development, Preservation, Organization, and Dissemination. When library practices get applied to firsthand accounts, those relevant stories become part of our known world and can improve public thought and action.

The instruction of Recognize, Record, Represent, and Reach has been concrete—in terms of steps to take—and also motivational (hopefully). Beyond just laying a path for action, this book's purpose is to highlight seminal principles that invigorate the discipline of librarianship. This chapter makes explicit those concepts, showing how they become brighter when oral history is the catalyst for their application. This chapter also reverberates with ideas proposed in R. David Lankes's *Atlas of New Librarianship*. Lankes's vision, as mapped in the *Atlas*, encompasses "learning, knowledge, and social action." No small scope! Fortunately, oral history provides a distinct lens through which to consider Lankes's sprawling picture; consequently, librarians have a view point and a vehicle for exercising the more inspirational aspects of our profession.

Forewarned is forearmed: This chapter is intended to provoke thought, and it therefore assumes a more philosophical tone. If conceptual musings are not your cup of tea, feel free to skip ahead to Chapter Six, which is entirely grounded. But do consider exploring the ideas presented here.

TOUCHSTONES

Information versus Entertainment

Instinctively, you might know the difference between subject matter intended to inform and matter formed primarily to entertain. But sometimes the line is blurred—especially when "story" gets involved. Entertainment, as described in *Merriam-Webster's*, occurs when something amusing or diverting is provided. The function is to shift attention, to provide a release from the strains of day-to-day work or rigor. Entertainment is necessary, and an amused public also can receive nourishment from recreational performances or displays. But the motivation for creating something in the realm of leisure, or pleasure, should not be confused with a motivation to inform.

If your library intends to or presently is conducting oral histories, be clear that what you are creating is information. Portions of interviews may be entertaining—narrators often tell stories that are humorously engaging—but the interview itself exists to enlighten public thought and action. Again, turning to *Merriam-Webster's*: Information is something (some type of message) that "justifies change in a construct" such as a plan or theory. Information is dynamic; it is characterized by movement of opinion and determination. The oral history provides the justification for altering whatever construct is resident within a particular listener or audience. This does not mean that oral history always makes people change their opinions. Rather, *oral history as information* is rich enough to warrant the possibility for change; a shift in actions or agenda reasonably could follow, on the basis of words spoken and experiences shared through oral recordings.

Libraries do an amazing job of stretching a capacity to provide and stimulate learning. With oral history, the narrator, interviewer, and audience must all grasp the end game: encouragement for learning. If community members are acting as interviewers, they need to value the product for its contribution to learning; the narrators must appreciate the role they play in creating new insights. At no time should anyone think of oral history as a diversion or amusement, even though parts of interviews can transport the imagination of the listener to an amusing location.

Maximum Accessibility

Think about the many ways your library works to ensure that all members of your community have access to resources. You meet the physical needs of the population by providing wheelchair ramps or elevators; you evaluate how people do their exploring and then make changes to your library landing page and make catalogs with facet searches; you offer e-books, books on CDs, and large-print volumes; and you supply reading rooms with comfy chairs and good lighting. If libraries formerly had a reputation for being aloof and uninviting (playing hard to get?), those days are past. The contemporary library will flex and bend to ensure ready entry for all the members of the community. And this same mindset must be applied to oral history.

The preceding chapter explained that an oral history is fully accessible only when it is discoverable, understandable, available, and usable. *Discoverable* means that people outside the library can learn of its existence without a preexisting awareness for its location or even its presence in the world. *Understandable* means that, once located, the informational content of the interview is made explicit in some fashion; people must know something about what is spoken during the oral history, in order to see that the interview is relevant to the query—or, at least, portions of the interview are in line with search criteria. *Available* means that the interview is positioned to be listened to, comparable to the readability of a book that is shelved in open stacks; the interview is not restricted and its content immediately can be delved. And finally, the oral history must exist in a format that makes its *use* possible. A cassette-tape interview without a cassette player is not usable; a transcript printed in a language not understood is not usable; a file format developed by a company and kept proprietary may not be "readable" by a majority of electronic devices, and therefore not usable. Discoverable, Understandable, Available, and Usable: If any of these links in the chain of accessibility breaks, the oral history is at risk for losing its audience—and, therefore, its purpose. (Senate historian Donald Ritchie often gets cited for his observation that "availability for research and reinterpretation defines oral history.")

As you begin to establish an oral history collection or, preferably, a program for ongoing interviews, make *accessibility* the cornerstone of your plan.

- Know exactly how interviews will surface, or what makes them surface when the public is searching for content.
- Identify the means by which interviews will be transcribed and/or described.
- Test the web platform that will be used for loading interview files.
- Stay abreast of product details that will influence the utility of forthcoming oral histories.

Retrofitting for desired outcomes is infinitely more onerous than careful planning. Be the future you want to see!

Content Grows in Meaning through Relationships

Have you had an experience like this: Someone tells you something that you had not previously heard, something new to you. Then, suddenly, that idea or topic or name starts surfacing *everywhere*. You can't turn around without someone mentioning "that thing." How had it escaped your attention? Under what rock has your awareness been shaded?

Connections are amorous—they like to multiply. A single attachment leads to another, and another, and another. And with each new connection, the original idea or topic becomes more comprehensible, more fulfilling. This outcome is central to the work of libraries. Bringing many different resources into proximity, the library creates conditions under which relationships can be observed. Occasionally, this happens as a matter of pure serendipity, like two books leaning against one another on a shelf. More often, the "accident" of discovery is achieved through rigorous organization.

Chapter Three focused on tactics that help an oral history to be understood, as it seeks its position to be found. And the same effort that facilitates discovery also conditions an interview for relation building. Descriptions applied to an oral history become connector nodes to other materials that share same or similar characteristics. A search term that brings up five different oral histories, as well as two articles and a book, tells you that those independent resources have something in common; then you might compare the content and glean new insights relevant to your initial query. Also helpful is seeing *quantity* in the identification of many different search returns; the number of results can be telling. The linked data movement aims to provide expansive connections between web-available objects and, consequently, extend the utility of any one item. Important to note: Structured approaches to data markup (e.g., BIBFRAME[1]), while excellent for *showing* relationships, cannot improve a general reception to the ideas, experiences, or stories of a resource. That type of relate-ability largely is determined by presentation.

With oral history, a person speaks on a subject about which he or she has specific knowledge and distinct understanding. Even when the topic is something broadly known—like the occurrence of a national disaster—the individual account brings focus, personality, and *reality*. The subject is made real through the voice of a person who speaks from firsthand experience. With community oral history, local voices explain the significance of timely events. And under these circumstances, the impact is further amplified. Imagine that your friend's brother is the one describing a particular event—or *your* brother. Does that increase the meaning or value? When community feels a relationship to the content, the resource has greater significance.

Grow relationships to the content.

So yes, work to establish connections between resources, to further demonstrate meaning. And also: Grow relationships to the content by making community voice a primary resource, by promoting oral history collections, and by providing inlets to the collection through events and programming.

THREADS

The Mission of Librarians Is to Improve Society through Facilitating Knowledge Creation in Their Communities[2]

I've already explained how R. David Lankes's *Atlas of New Librarianship* tugged my imagination for what librarians' purpose can be, and how oral history can be a providential library function. What follows are points taken from *The Atlas* and offered in the context of oral history as a library pursuit. No attempt is made to summarize, explain, or confront the assertions of Lankes's full text. But the central ingredient of his *Atlas*, the mission statement, is primary grist for extended thinking.

Knowledge

Where is the Life we have lost in living?
Where is the wisdom we have lost in knowledge?
Where is the knowledge we have lost in information?[3]

T. S. Eliot, in *The Rock*—through no strategic intent—drafted a poetic precursor to Ackoff's DIKW pyramid, which surfaces throughout the literature and curriculum of library and information studies. Ackoff's continuum (briefly mentioned in Chapter Three) suggests an improvement or refinement of output that occurs between stages of exposure to data, to information, to knowledge, and on to wisdom. The model, while aspirational, does not directly speak to ways of accelerating the process; that chore is left to people like David Lankes—and to you.

Knowledge, according to *Merriam-Webster's*, is an "awareness or familiarity gained by experience of a fact or situation." Knowledge has two parts: encountering and absorbing. When you know something, that something—usually information—has taken hold and planted roots; it can be felt. Accepting Lankes's mission statement, your role is to facilitate "knowing" in your community, and you do so by setting ideal conditions.

Knowledge Is Created through Conversation

The USC Shoah Foundation hosts an archive of over 50,000 testimonies from individuals who are survivors of or witnesses to genocides, predominantly the Holocaust. The audiovisual recordings are catalogued and indexed and some are made available through an online portal—an incredible, daunting, and gripping composite of firsthand experiences. Interviews can be used to engage a public audience in formal and informal education, to explain the impact of genocide from the voices of those with intimate knowledge. The existing archive is an unparalleled resource—still, the Shoah Foundation is pushing the boundaries of innovation, exploring the use of holograms to create new conversation opportunities. The project is called New Dimensions in Testimony; it allows people to ask questions of a projected image of an interviewee, who responds to individual queries, just as would happen if two *real* humans were sitting together in dialogue.[4] Of course, the expenditure of time and technology to make this happen is mind numbing—not remotely possible for an average library. But the reasoning behind the Shoah Foundation's investment is instructive: "Having a one on one conversation with someone remains one of the most immersive experiences a human being can share."[5] Knowing that at some point no Holocaust survivors will be alive to dialogue with others, the Shoah Foundation wants to recreate that opportunity for next generations.

Knowledge is not some artifact or item, but rather a uniquely human resource arrived at through active conversation. (Lankes 2011, 29)

You don't need to achieve a high level of sophistication to realize the benefit of conversational learning. Chapter Two talks about the traits of an excellent oral history interviewer—the preparation and skill that make for an exceptional oral history recording. A really good interviewer is able to ask questions that would be on the minds of outside listeners. People who have a favorite radio host often say: "Jane Radio Host asks the questions that I want to pose." For the interviewer, this means putting aside assumptions and instead being open to the details as they emerge. Follow-up questions are asked not for the benefit of the interviewer but for the clarification provided to external listeners. The best interviewer is an advocate for the future; future audiences should feel a proxy participation in the dialogue. Participation heightens the learning experience for someone trying to grasp the meaning of whatever is being discussed.

Finally, think about how conversations are scalable. With a collection of interviews that are focused on the same topic, the goal is to document a full mix of viewpoints that surround the subject being explored. Competing viewpoints, placed in proximity to one another, create the conditions for dialogue—you hear conversation among the voices of the collection. Over time, this dynamic invites the collection to grow in meaning even when the quantity of interviews stops increasing.

Knowledge Is a Web of Personal Truths

During the course of an oral history, I recorded a woman speaking about the experience of canvassing for a political candidate who incited great passions from a great many folks across the political spectrum and in the milieu of public opinion. A particular incident stood out. The canvasser knocked on a door, and when a woman answered, the canvasser explained why she was there—who she was representing:

There was a woman, I had knocked on her door. She was older. She was prob-
ably in her sixties or so. When I told her that I was with the _____ campaign,
she said some pretty nasty things. She said: "I wouldn't vote for that" and she
used the N-word "if he was the last person on earth." So, I just said Thank
You. She closed the door. And as I was walking down the stairs, she opened
the door back up. And she said: "You know, it's a really hot day out there."
She goes: "Would you like to come in for some lemonade?" So I said, "Sure.
You know, I would. I would love to come in for some lemonade." So, I did.
We were talking about our kids; I was asking her about her kids. We just small
talked. . . . Then, as I was leaving, she apologized to me. She said, "You know,
the way that I reacted—I'm embarrassed about." And I said . . . "You know
what, the fact that you opened that door, and you asked me to come back
in—that speaks volumes of what this whole thing should be about."[6]

In Chapter One you learned about Studs Terkel's encounters with narrators who hear themselves for the first time—the woman who clasps her hand
to her mouth: "Oh my God," she says. "I never knew I felt that way before."
In the above excerpt, you hear a telling of that same experience from a
slightly different angle: The woman behind the door comes to a personal
truth, a moment of knowing herself, after her interaction with the canvasser—after she realizes what she has said. That moment turned out to be
equally powerful for the woman whom I later recorded, who wanted to
share the experience, to talk about it and process the meaning for herself.

Knowledge is created through conversation. And conversation reveals
personal truths that allow "we the people" to better understand ourselves
and one another. Thoughts and feelings season and evolve. Oral history
allows an individual to express ideas and opinions that have accumulated
over time, and through recorded interviews, community can hear iterations
of learning that are the closest approximation of what a person *now* holds
as certainty.

Memory Enriches Current Conversations

When people are taking photographs or collecting memorabilia, you may
hear the expression: "This is for history." However, the reason for preserving and making available recorded experiences is not historical—the reason
is contemporary. By exploring what has transpired in the past, present-day
situations are better contextualized and understood. Sometimes, the comparison between past and present reveals great progress; other times, the les-
son is scolding—a remembered point in history may show that current
behavior is a devolution. *Having* memory as a leverage point is the important
thing. Narrator Pinchas Gutter's composite testimonials were used for Shoah
Foundation's test hologram. In a follow-up interview, Gutter says:
"Genocide like the Holocaust should be taught by the people who suffered
it, who experienced it, and who can give people a feeling for the way it really

was."[7] That richness of experience is valuable only when it is brought into current dialogue, to inform new conversations.

By grounding libraries in knowledge, we gain an inheritance not of quiet bookishness but of explosive power to shape how people see the world. (Lankes 2011, 31)

Facilitation

You want knowledge to grow and expand for your community, but you don't get there by yourself becoming smarter or more informed or chock-full of understanding. You need to encourage and expedite that for your community members; that single function is the soul of librarianship. ILS maintenance, materials acquisition, databases subscriptions, skills instruction, makerspace hours, and lecture series—as examples—all assist knowledge transfer. So, too, does something simple like retrieving a book and handing it to a community member. Or, helping a member learn to read. The grounds for creating knowledge are fertile, and oral history is poised to occupy a parcel of that lush territory. How do you make it happen?

Shared Ownership: With, Not For

Chapter One, Recognize, covers collection development. Sometimes, that function gets boiled down to algorithms and metrics assessments, but truly, the building of resources is much more personal and communal. Books are not acquired *for* the community, they are acquired with the community in mind. Equally, every other type of resource joins the library collection because members show interest or curiosity. Charles Leadbeater writes and speaks extensively on innovation and creativity. In 2009, he drafted an essay titled "The Art of With," which discusses different emotional outcomes that flow from experiences of *For, To,* or *With*. Leadbeater explains that sometimes having things done for you—while sounding generous—translates to an experience of infliction, more like having something done *to* you. Leadbeater says: "The world of To and For starts from people as bundles of needs, rather than, say, as bundles of capabilities and potential."

If members do not participate, they are not learning. It is they who are allowing us to participate in their learning. (Lankes 2011, 65)

Oral history, as a library function, recognizes community members precisely for their capabilities and potential. An oral history collection tells community: *You possess experiences and ideas and understandings that can benefit others. The library values you; the library sees YOU as a community resource.* Is this exploitation? Barely. Or, maybe it's an invitation for mutual investment that pays dividends to both parties. Community members can suggest topics to be explored through interviews or suggest people whose experiences need to be understood. Or, members can suggest themselves as experts on a given topic. Someone might have a research interest that is not addressed through existing published materials; this creates an opportunity for that individual to conduct interviews that become part of the library. Participation is the name of the game.

Publishers of Community

To varying degrees, libraries always have been involved in publishing. Think about it. One definition of "publish" is to communicate or disseminate, which clearly is central to the existence of libraries as resource hubs. A more predominant understanding involves responsibility for issuing forth (e.g., printing), along with preparations for that outcome. Libraries traditionally have been less invested in that latter type of publishing, though by no means absent. In recent years, exemplary models have emerged from a variety of library settings, such as Massachusetts's Provincetown Public Library, which created its own imprint.[8] Noticeably, the discussion of "library as publisher" has emphasized a product—print or electronic— created by a local author with assistance and support from the library. The resulting text can be sold in addition to being cataloged, shelved, and circulated. A different spin on this idea is "Library as Publisher of Community," without an objective to create something physical, or to sell anything, but merely to "make known." Choosing to bring oral history into your library, making oral history a part of your dedicated mission, you become a publisher of community. Earlier in this chapter, I talked about the distinction between entertainment and information, explicitly stating that oral history is created to inform. Individuals in your community possess knowledge that can inform public thought and action *because* you have taken responsibility for seeing that it gets "issued forth." At a macro level, the collection of oral histories can also communicate your local population to a larger, outside demographic. You are giving others access to your community. Imagine this as a shining opportunity to present local knowledge—local personality—on a grander stage.

> *I foresee the day ... where acquisition is a matter of production, not purchasing. The future of libraries (and librarians) is in becoming publishers of the community.* (Lankes 2011, 67)

Space for Community Identification

When somebody comes to the library looking for a resource, your role as a librarian is to assist the discovery process. Typically, this involves locating materials, identifying online content, or compiling references. The dance is one of search and discovery. Wouldn't it be magnificent if people came to the library to find strength? If you could help them discover empowerment? Both of these circumstances are possible when the library is a place that showcases community members—where they see themselves reflected.

True and successful facilitation is when a librarian helps a member find his or her own story. (Lankes 2011, 87)

Building a collection of oral histories alongside other library resources puts those firsthand experiences on par with traditional, legitimized documentation. Exposing the knowledge of community members releases the power of those voices. Connection is what you offer; this is a core strength of the library. Members must know that *what* they own as an experience is important to the library—important enough to make it visible via the discovery tools that libraries wield. Make your library a place where community says: *I helped to create this organization; I am part of this library; I see myself; this is where I belong.* Whether or not these words come from the lips of community members, this feeling must be present. Create the circumstances where, literally, people find their own story—their own recorded interview, their own voice.

Improving Society

The highest stage of the DIKW pyramid is Wisdom. In each person, the accumulation and processing of data, information, and knowledge—along with a state of understanding—can lead to a level of wisdom. Rather, *might* lead to a level of wisdom. Wisdom is demonstrated through actions. The evidence of wisdom is shown when knowledge and understanding are used to achieve an outcome that is well judged and, presumably, most effective and beneficial in consequence.[9]

Lankes's mission statement places the improvement of society as the focused goal of a librarian's work. Not simply distributing information, or being present when information is sought; the goal is specific to an outcome that sounds very much like "increased wisdom." This is excellent news, because the work of oral history—ensuring the existence of conversations—is a step down this path. Conversations are shown to build knowledge that can influence improved decision making. Still, one additional factor merits consideration: your personal role and your responsibility for demonstrating the values of wisdom. What are the behavioral hallmarks that you can be working toward, leveraging oral history?

Openness

Chapter One has a sample planning grid, depicting how a collection of interviews, topically focused, might start being organized. The idea is to ensure a thorough coverage of the issues as well as the perspectives related to a given subject. While the planning grid itself is preconceived and highly calculated, the information gleaned from the project—the content of the oral histories—may come as a surprise. More pointedly, the content *should* offer unexpected insights. In many instances, the stories that come from different narrators will rub against one another, showing disagreement about areas seemingly rooted in fact. And sometimes, the viewpoints will be not only discordant but also discomforting or inflammatory.

> *We gain trust by consistently giving members a variety of sources and perspectives.* (Lankes 2011, 92)

The freedom of individual narrators to speak their own truths must be upheld in the same way that librarians defend the principles of intellectual freedom. The determination of what is "good" or "bad" does not come from you; that judgement is left to the audience of listeners. Your responsibility is to ensure a *good experience* for community members who lend their perspectives, and those who apply their attention toward the oral histories. Establishing a culture of respect around "community voice" is exactly within the purview of your responsibility and professional integrity.

Innovation

In 2017, the Association of College and Research Libraries (ACRL) titled their conference *At the Helm: Leading Transformation*. One of the papers presented during those proceedings came from Holly Hendrigan, of Simon Fraser University Library. Hendrigan's contribution was titled "Naturals with a Microphone: Oral History and the Librarian Skillset" and was inspired by Martha Jane K. Zachert, mentioned in Chapter Two.
But consider the full chain of inspiration:

1. In 1948, historian Allen Nevins staged the first interview archive at the Oral History Research Office, Columbia University.
2. In the 1960s, the existence of reel-to-reel tape recorders made the practice of oral history more widespread, and in 1967, Columbia University hosted the Second Oral History Colloquium; Zachert attended that meeting and was excited by the "creative opportunity," with the implication that librarians could/should be instigators of oral history and position themselves as interviewers.
3. In 1968, Zachert described her ideas in an article titled "The Implications of Oral History for Librarians."

Flash forward nearly 50 years, and you have Holly Hendrigan revitalizing Zachert's sentiments and making her assertions contemporary. Hendrigan conducted interviews in a project documenting the historical relationship between the Technical College of British Columbia and Simon University, Surrey (the TechBC Memory Project). At the conclusion of her work, Hendrigan engaged in "autoethnography" to describe and analyze her experience—explaining that "no librarian has yet applied autoethnography to the oral history interview process." Within the published paper, a reader encounters the moment when Hendrigan is bitten with certainty that oral history should be in the domain of librarians—should be engaged by more librarians. Oral history naturally belongs to *you*, as much as anyone. Hendrigan's excursion with interviewing arose from a professional development opportunity. Before advancing with the project, she had to conquer her own insecurities as a self-taught oral historian, and then further expose herself by examining/critiquing the experience.

My self reflection process began with Alessandro Portelli, one of oral history's preeminent scholars.... Responding to critics who questioned the credibility of memories, he argued "[t]he importance of oral testimony may lie not in its adherence to fact, but rather in its departure from it, as imagination, symbolism and desire emerge." Portelli thus changed the conversation surrounding oral history from facts to meaning. (Hendrigan 2017)

Fascinating to be reminded that oral history, as a form of documentation, itself had to overcome an insecurity about its worthiness! For Hendrigan, the effort paid off—as is the case so often with anything novel and exploratory. And you can find similar reward. Whether or not you choose to be an oral historian, you must be an advocate for the placement of oral history in your library.

All too often we see innovation as having to fundamentally change the world when it only has to improve your life. (Lankes 2011, 127)

Being Human

Oral history, the oldest and most enduring form of information transfer, can elevate the practice of librarianship in service to cultural heritage and community involvement. The process of recording a person's story validates that individual's experience and elevates his or her self-worth. Taking it a step further: Connecting individuals to the true experiences of other persons creates a picture of reality that is grounded in imagination for the "other." Better decisions come from better understanding, and better decisions improve lives. With oral history, the power (a.k.a., knowledge) is resident in the community, in individual members—but responsibility for assisting the spread of knowledge, extending the conversation, is personal to the individual librarian.

Humanities scholars understand the idea of the society as a grand conversation taking place over all of human history. (Lankes 2011, 176)

FINISHING THOUGHTS

This chapter highlights many ideas, concepts, precepts, and practices—time-tested and fresh—that can inspire you to bring oral history into your library. Paraphrasing David Lankes:

- Librarianship is about outcomes and learning, not materials
- Librarians are rewarded for improvements facilitated, not items collected
- Libraries must invest in the tools of creation over the products of acquisition

These are statements as well as prompts. Action is up to you—movement is up to you. Any library is poised to be a publisher of community, because every library reflects a body of individuals who have a voice. No library—or library setting—is immune to the power and potential of oral history's invigorating character.

NOTES

1. BIBRAME (Bibliographic Framework) is being developed by the Library of Congress, to transition away from MARC format and to take advantage of Linked Data concepts. It is conceived as a "foundation for the future of bibliographic description." https://www.loc.gov/bibframe/.

2. R. David Lankes, *The Atlas of New Librarianship* (Cambridge, MA: The MIT Press, 2011). Lankes offers a mission statement that is the organizing principle for his presentation of concepts. The mission statement ("improve society through facilitating knowledge creation") is repeated and reiterated throughout the pages of the *Atlas*.

3. T. S. Eliot, *The Rock: A Pageant Play* (London: Faber & Faber, 1934). T. S. Eliot did not consider himself the author of the play, only "of the words." The first scene opens with a chorus, speaking "as the voice of the Church of God." The excerpt about information, knowledge, and wisdom comes from these opening words.

4. New Dimensions in Testimony: "A collection of interactive biographies from USC Shoah Foundation that enable people to have conversations with pre-recorded video images of Holocaust survivors and other witnesses to genocide." Web link: https://sfi.usc.edu/collections/holocaust/ndt.

5. https://creators.vice.com/en_us/article/d749xk/holocaust-survivors-hologram-testimonies.

6. This is one of a number of interviews I conducted in 2008, documenting the experience of individuals who had volunteered for the Obama campaign in a district that historically was *deep* red. Narrators in the project signed a consent to share their oral histories for education purposes, as I deemed suitable.

7. https://www.fastcompany.com/40427922/so-we-never-forget-holograms-will-keep-delivering-first-person-holocaust-survivor-testimony (article 6-20-2017).

8. James LaRue writes about "Library as Publisher" in an article for *American Libraries*, June 25, 2013. Also in 2013, successful projects were launched by the Provincetown Public Library (MA) and the Williams County Public Library (TN),

as described in a *Library Journal* article, March 26, 2014, "The Public Library as Publisher." That article concludes with a response to the question: Can Any Library Do This?

9. Russell Ackoff, "From Data to Wisdom," *Journal of Applied Systems Analysis*, 1989, vol. 16, pp. 3–9. My thoughts are determined largely through interpretations of Ackoff's model, coupled with my own musings.

6

Reality and Rewards

Oral history should be exercised in any library setting. At the same time, having a picture of *one* location can be broadly instructive. This chapter draws upon experiences at the Boulder Public Library (BPL), and the Maria Rogers Oral History Program (MROHP), to illustrate a "proof of concept" for the areas covered in Chapters One through Four: Recognize, Record, Represent, and Reach. The objective is to show a tested path that can help you find *your* path. As with any new endeavor, trial and error are part of the journey. Perhaps one day you will be contributing to a lessons-learned publication.

Also, this chapter talks about the return on investment that comes with choosing oral history as an activity of the library. Interviews do not guarantee that money will arrive on your doorstep—but the rewards of making shelf space for voice are distinctly lucrative.

COLLECTION DEVELOPMENT: RECOGNIZE

Collection development is guided by the situation of the library—sometimes the building, literally—and the changing priorities of the community. For example, the Carnegie Library for Local History is a branch of the BPL; the Carnegie building was the community's original public library, and the iconic structure became the sole destination for BPL's collection of county-centered materials. Oral histories started being gathered as early as 1976, via cassette tapes. Coinciding with the library's emergence as a repository for local history, a volunteer named Maria Rogers came forward to manage the oral history efforts, growing the quantity of interviews as well as the number of community oral historians—all volunteers. After Maria died, an endowment ensured the continuity of the oral history program.

Collection development for oral histories is consistent with Carnegie's overall mission of documenting the social history of Boulder County. Staff acquires resources that create a full picture of the geography, demography, times, politics, and social and physical landscape of Boulder County. Interviews fall into the two categories of "Person" and "Topic." Individual citizens may be identified for a depth of knowledge or enduring contribution to the community; those people would be interviewed to get an understanding of their personal history. Or, a specific subject might be identified as historically relevant, and then community members with knowledge of that subject are sought for interviewing.

In addition to specifying appropriate interview content, the library makes explicit the meaning of "oral history interview," compared to other types of recordings or journalistic endeavors. This becomes important when people want to donate interviews, or when people will be conducting interviews for their own purposes and would consider making a donation if their approach can be compatible with the goals and boundaries of oral history interviewing.

Need and Opportunity

You will discover that *need* and *opportunity* surface again and again throughout any practical discussion of oral history. The occasion for an interview does not arrive out of boredom; something motivates the application of time and attention and the preparation that goes into an interview. Either you will be compelled into the effort or a situation will be too compelling to forgo.

The best scenario for launching an oral history project is one in which need and opportunity come together as impetus. Since oral documentation relies on the vivacity of individual narrators—a person being alive *and* being capable of cogently sharing recollections—the timeliness of catching a person must be considered. The same is true for projects of topical focus, where a situation is evolving rapidly, and the rawness of emotion is valued equal to the crispness of detail.

For example, when Boulder experienced unprecedented flooding in 2013, the historical significance of the occasion immediately was apparent. The library knew that documentation of the flood would be part of a future collection and the opportunity to conduct interviews in the near aftermath, when recollections were vivid, was a fleeting window. The existence of MROHP—with leadership, volunteers, equipment, and protocols—allowed a project to coalesce with effective speed. The result is a set of interviews with residents, first responders, government officials, and others—all gathered quickly after the event. At a future date (e.g., on the occasion of the ten-year anniversary), more interviews can be conducted, to demonstrate changes in public opinion, planning, or perspective. Interviews that are more reflective in nature will supplement those that were reflexive. The takeaway: An oral history collection is realized when you act on moments of opportunity, whatever the associated event.

Complementing Other Resources

Your library's predictable offerings—regardless of scope, content, and format—can be enhanced by the addition of oral history. The Carnegie Library, as a home for local history, gathers documents (diaries, letters, personal and organizational papers), maps, photographs, newspapers and clippings, books (authored titles as well as phone books and year books), and periodicals. Pamphlets, brochures, and ephemera, in addition to genealogical indices, directories, and other records, round out the catalog. One element not mentioned in this rich and diverse collection is voice. Recordings are best for capturing the *living personality* of the community.

Reference staff often have the best vantage for suggesting whom to interview, as they have a comprehensive awareness for what exists and what is lacking. In one instance at BPL, a family approached the library with historic photos of a home that was one of the first built in a particular neighborhood, a landmark structure. Through conversation, staff learned that the matriarch of the family was still living . . . and still living in the original house! This presented a wonderful opportunity to record an interview. Now, the donated photos can be brought to life by stories that come from the rooms, hallways, and front walk of the family home. Yes, sometimes pictures can talk.

Collaborations and Partnerships

Key relationships can help initiate, sustain, and improve a body of interviews. For example, Boulder County Open Space and Mountain Parks (OSMP) had interest in capturing the oral histories of individuals whose land would be designated for open space preservation. This would be a way to recognize the individuals and their families and get the history of the properties. Library staff provided interview training; the two organizations drafted a joint-release form; and oral histories from that project, ongoing, are shared with the Carnegie Library. Completed interviews have become part of a special collection documenting the open-space movement and the acquisition of land.

Another example comes with the Boulder County Latino History Project.[1] Researchers realized that contributions from Boulder's Latino population largely were absent from public awareness and the history curriculum in local schools. With the application of rigorous planning, a multiyear project included the taping of just over 40 oral histories with individuals from the Latino community—interviews conducted by interns within the project. These oral histories were added to the Carnegie archive, and existing interviews with Latinos and Latinas—dating back to the late seventies—were redressed and made more accessible, with fresh transcripts in some cases. Other resources were created or rejuvenated for the project, which resulted in a trove of research material published via a website and a two-volume book set.

Engaging Community

The work of *locals' history* can be a centerpiece for other community engagement and enrichment endeavors: adult programming, youth services, and periodic exhibits. With an oral history program, citizen participation is imperative; nothing can be added to the collection, nothing can be accomplished, without direct engagement. Community members are tapped in order to acquire names of potential interviewees and topics to be explored. Ideas regularly come from members—members can submit a recommendation form, call the library, email, or stop over to make a suggestion. Each of these occasions is an opportunity to point out the voices already preserved and the range of topics explored.

As an example: The Carnegie Library received a call from someone whose friend had been interviewed as one of the "founding mothers" of the Jewish Community Center preschool. The caller wondered if the library might be interested in getting the recordings of the founders of Boulder Hospice, which was about to celebrate a milestone anniversary. Indeed, this presented as a wonderful opportunity, and recordings of four seminal figures were obtained. Sometime after that, one of the interviewees and a friend came to the library—the first time either one had set foot in the building—and asked to learn more about the library, the oral history program, and the archive of voices. For more than an hour, the two received details and received instruction on accessing the online interviews. They discovered that several acquaintances had been interviewed, and they learned how to search for more content from their personal devices.

Library volunteers also suggest interviews and do the work of orchestrating whole projects. Over the years, volunteers have spearheaded special collections on subject matter including the farmers market, the school district, the practice of Buddhism in Boulder, the experience of homelessness, and the Rocky Flats nuclear weapons plant.

Finishing thoughts on *Recognize*: Chapter One's purpose was to describe an evolution of awareness that makes oral history a central function of library activity. Equally important is the revelation of what librarians can do *with* oral history, to bring together voices, perspectives, and truths, to build a comprehensive picture of reality.

PRESERVATION: RECORD

Capturing Voice

Format Options and Equipment

Oral history succeeds when opportunity is recognized, the record button is pressed, and the personal knowledge of an individual is made known to the community. With Carnegie's earliest interviews dating back to the late

1970s, audio was being used for oral history. The library still has shelves of original cassette tapes, even as tapes have been digitized and WAV and MP3 files created. In the late 1990s, when video started gaining traction and became more popular, the library invested in video cameras that stored recordings to mini DV tapes (digital video cassette tapes). Between 1997 and 2015, the majority of oral histories for MROHP were conducted as video, and for much of that time, the oral history program was extraordinary for pioneering into "moving image" format.

However, the choice to emphasize video did have its costs. Literally, the dollar figure for maintaining cameras, tapes, batteries, microphones, cables and connectors, tripods, and so on could be expensive. Also, the time expenditure for monitoring and keeping stock of all the moving parts was measurable. And after interviews were completed, the mini DV tapes had to be run through a conversion process to burn DVDs, because common devices do not play mini DV tapes. As a last step, audio files were created from the DVDs, to allow compressed electronic storage, preservation, and online streaming.

In 2015, the oral history program gave new thought to the capture of interviews and shifted back to audio as the primary format. Three digital audio recorders were purchased (Zoom H2n), along with one digital video camera (Zoom Q8). The factors that weighed into this decision are as follows:

- The library's goal for oral history is to create enduring information, and that goal is accomplished with audio.
- Video does not have an agreed upon preservation format (file options are highly proprietary), whereas WAV is standard and ubiquitous for audio and therefore more sustainable.
- At different times, storage for video has not been assured, as the file size can be ten times that of audio.
- The vast majority of interviews conducted for MROHP involve a single person talking for a lengthy period of time (a.k.a., the "talking head"). No reason compels this type of video; the idea of showing a person can be accomplished with one photograph.
- Interviews are used for research and education, where parts of an interview are identified—via transcript, typically—and those parts might be excerpted.
- The staging of interviews for audio, versus video, is much simpler and often more comfortable for both the interviewer and the narrator.
- The operation of audio equipment (especially with the Zoom H2n) is simple and can produce excellent sound.
- The storage capacity for an SD card allows many interviews to be conducted with no worry of running out of tape.
- In the instance when an oral history involves a demonstration, or other reason for seeing the interview, the digital video camera is available.

- While YouTube remains popular for certain types of videos as well as short pieces, the platforms for audio creations (e.g., podcasts) are drawing youthful and professional audiences.

To boil things down: Look for the sweet spot of quality, simplicity, and utility—with an eye toward cost and durability—considering the needs and abilities of participants, the resulting workflow, and mindful of purpose. Decisions should be commensurate with library goals, which differ from those of oral history producers who come from commercial or other settings.

Participants Identified

Suggestion forms are excellent for inviting the community to recommend people for interview. Carnegie's form requires contact information for the potential narrator as well as the person who is making the suggestion, an explanation of why the person should be interviewed, and a description of topics that might be covered during an oral history. Also, the form asks if the interview has specific urgency—this could be an awareness for the person's advancing age or deteriorating health. On many occasions, recommendations arrive ad hoc—an email or phone call. A running list tracks potential narrators, along with the date of recommendation. This list gets pushed out to volunteers who have made themselves available to conduct interviewers.

The library never guarantees that any person who has been suggested will have an oral history. Library staff can be persuasive in pushing interviewers toward certain individuals, when the reason for interview is highly compelling, but no guarantees are offered. Volunteers who spearhead their own projects are responsible for identifying their narrators. Again, library staff can be instructive in helping volunteers think about the types of perspectives that should be captured, as well as who might represent those perspectives.

Volunteers themselves reach the library through different inroads. A coordinator for all of BPL monitors applications and acts as a matchmaker between likely candidates and the oral history program. Volunteers who want to become interviewers receive training from the MROHP coordinator—though training in oral history techniques might be acquired from other sources in the community, and skills can be passed on from one volunteer to another. Newcomers to the program might participate in an interview as a notetaker—notetakers do not engage in the conversation but write down topics, place names, and person names that come up during the recording. This is a great way to ease someone new into the process and create familiarity with the discipline of conducting an oral history.

Staging the Interview

Chapter Two outlined the factors influencing your decision about where to locate the oral history interview. For many years, conducting interviews in the homes of narrators was commonplace and the default choice for MROHP. When interviewers and narrators know one another, this still might happen. But now the default is for the interview to take place in a public location that offers a quiet space protected from intrusion—preferably one of BPL's meeting or study rooms. Over time, this approach creates more continuity in the "soundscape" and makes the blending of excerpts more seamless.

The interviewer is responsible for contacting the oral history coordinator and reserving recording equipment for checkout. MROHP has three recorders available, each including an accessory pack with all of the necessary staging elements: extension cord; extra batteries; a small tripod stand; and a remote control for starting, stopping, and pausing the recording. Also included are copies of the release form, and a cheat sheet for operating the recorder—though each device has been prepped, so pressing *record* is nearly all that's required.

In advance of the oral history date, the interviewer will discuss the process with the narrator and make sure that expectations are in line. After the interview, equipment and release are returned to library, and the coordinator checks to ensure that all elements are present. At BPL, interviewers do nothing with the audio file saved on the recorder—file transfer is left to the coordinator.

Becoming a Steward of the Recording

Stewardship has four key ingredients: care, responsibility, trust, and management. If you establish an oral history program, position it to be a worthy steward of the community's firsthand experiences. In Boulder, the library and the Library Foundation have shown ongoing commitment by assisting the MROHP endowment: small grants for new equipment and special projects, desk and work space (including computers), room and shelf space, IT support, reference support, and creative encouragement (web and graphic design, exhibit help). With the backing of your library—with an enduring belief in the program—you will succeed as a caretaker of community voice.

Release Forms and Documentation

As stated previously, release forms are absolutely required for all interviews, and further documentation is beneficial. You can construct a release that meets the particular goals of your library; MROHP recently updated its standard form to include language consistent with the Creative Commons "Attribution Non-Commercial" license. This is commensurate with the library's mission to allow and encourage use of material, as long as the primary purpose is not commercial and always with credit to the library. Interviewees do not give away the right to use their own interviews;

interviewees can exercise personal decision about what they do with their own recording, including a commercial use.

The release further explains that the library will make interviews publicly available, and the library expects that interviews will be accessed for education, exhibition, programming, and documentary production—as examples of outcomes. When the form is returned to the library, it is coded with a unique identifier (more on this later) and placed into a three-ring binder that is organized alphabetically by narrators' last names. The library also now scans the release forms and saves them as PDF files.

A tracking sheet is started for every oral history that comes into the library. The sheet starts with a "call number" (unique identifier) and lists all of the steps that will move the interview from its nascent form to a completed project. For all intents and purposes, every interview is a project, as every interview must be translated into derivative copies (e.g., MP3 file or transcript), described, saved to multiple locations, integrated into the library's OPAC, and loaded to the library website. Different people—mostly volunteers, mostly working distantly—contribute to stages of each interview's progression; for this reason, the library is exploring dynamic means for tracking and updating the progress of each oral history. (Trello is an example of a dynamic, web-based application that might work for the library.) Carefully think through the steps you will be taking and evaluate the most convenient and functional tool for documenting your oral history endeavors—a well-constructed spreadsheet might be all that you require.

File Structuring and Continuity of Collection

A tracking slip, spreadsheet, or workflow software helps keep a process organized, but *actions* ensure that interviews become an enduring part of your library's commitment to community. At the Carnegie Library, when the recorder is returned, the program coordinator checks in the oral history and assigns a unique identifier. The interview collection starts with OH0001, and at the time of this writing is up to OH2070. The coordinator then moves the audio file from the recorder to a folder on the oral history work station (backed up by city IT); that file, a WAV, is *copied* to an external hard drive designated specifically for oral history. Also, cloud storage is being arranged for the library's comprehensive digital assets—and this will be the archive that is the third and most well-protected location for all of the preservation WAV copies. From files saved to the external hard drive, MP3 "working" copies can be created. These MP3s might be tweaked for presentation, compressed for sharing over the Internet, and so on.

The library keeps one electronic folder for WAV, one for MP3, one for transcripts, one for summaries, one for photos, and so on. Over time, MROHP—with different staff and different ideas—has employed different naming conventions for different files associated with interviews. And yes, that's a lot of "differents." The variation in approach has posed challenges at times when the library needs to access files or is trying to sort files or migrate files from one format to another. Fortunately, with every instance—WAV, MP3, MOV, transcript, and summary—the file name has included that unique OH identifier. This has meant that the library can associate files with one another, regardless of *what* the oral history format is.

Every person who has been part of MROHP over the years has cared deeply about the program and has made decisions with the good of the program in mind. In addition to cassette tapes, shelves hold rows of gold DVDs that, when they were created, were thought to be the gold standard for ensuring the longevity of a recording. While practices have changed as new understandings have emerged, those shining discs still can be seen— as a reminder of the enduring passion that has been committed over the years.

ORGANIZATION: REPRESENT

In 2005, an article by Mark Greene and Dennis Meissner appeared in the Fall/Winter issue of the journal *The American Archivist*. Greene and Meissner advocated an approach to resource management dubbed "More Product, Less Process" (MPLP),[2] suggesting that professionals should do the minimum to make content available to the public—something closer to pulling a box out of storage and setting it in a reading room. The very real starting point for that proposal was the known backlog of unprocessed materials sitting in archives across the country.

I can empathize with the worry of a large backlog. However, for oral history, that predicament needs to be addressed first with "Less Product" in the sense of being concerted, thoughtful, and intentional when planning interview projects; maybe less should be created in the first place. Then, spend "more" on the time-intensive work of processing an oral history, demonstrating the attributes of each interview. Spending more time on processing does command a large portion of hours resources—and the expenditure is worth it. You cannot expect the public to listen to an interview if they don't understand what the content holds.

Creating Access Points to the Audio

Transcription

As a person who has spent considerable time mining interview collections to find specific first-person experiences, I deeply appreciate the value of a transcript. Surprisingly, MROHP has had lots of people offer to help with this kind of work, which allows volunteers to contribute to the library from home or elsewhere during any hours of the day. People enjoy learning about the community and appreciate the challenge of representing voice in text—the art of bridging that transition. The key is to provide a guidelines document that instructs on all of the how-to details.

When a volunteer is ready to work on a transcript, the MROHP coordinator emails the oral history's audio file as well as the start to the document, which is a template that has been partially filled in with names and dates, and so on. TransferBigFiles.com can be used to send audio; occasionally, a long interview will need to have its sound file compressed to meet the size restriction of TransferBigFile's free service. (Of course, this should be done only with a working copy and never to the original.)

When volunteers complete the transcript, it is emailed back to the coordinator. A downside to using volunteers is the uncertainty of when a completed transcript will be returned. You can't, after all, demand a deadline. You might also find variation in the accuracy and style of transcripts produced by different people. The plus side includes the word *free*, as transcription services can be costly. Also, a strong and positive connection is created when volunteers do the work. This connection extends between the library and the volunteer; also, the transcriber, interviewer, and narrator are now bonded—even when they haven't met!

All of the transcripts should be reviewed by a second set of eyes and ears. Typically the coordinator will be this second person, but volunteers who are well-seasoned and have an enduring relationship with the library might be utilized in this role. After the transcript has been audited, the completed document gets emailed to the narrator, and that person has the opportunity to correct errors or fill in words that were not understood by either the transcriber or the auditor. In the text of the email, very specific language explains the purpose of the review:

> *Attached you will find a transcript of your interview with JANE DOE. I would be glad to have you read it over and alert me to any <u>factual</u> or <u>typographical</u> errors, such as misspelled words or names, or incorrect dates. The goal is to have the transcript match the spoken conversation of your interview, because the transcript will be offered as the audio is being played through our online archive. <u>Note</u>: Nothing is to be edited or rewritten; we value the orality of the interview and identify the original recording as the primary source. The transcript helps researchers identify specific portions of interest and then listen to those segments.*

With this explanation, the library has had good luck with narrators offering necessary and helpful changes but not trying to edit the transcript in the way of magazine interviews that are heavily reworked. Narrators are told that if two weeks pass and no response is given, the library will proceed with publishing the interview; also, narrators are instructed to contact the library at any point if concerns arise.

Further Description and Metadata

When you have a short interview, or one that lacks detailed substance, a summary might suffice in lieu of a transcript for showing the contents of an interview. Summaries involve time stamps and descriptions of what was being talked about at those points in time. This approach is extremely sensible and can be effective. The summary can be created much more quickly than a transcript; it doesn't need to be perfect, and it doesn't require narrator review.

For all interviews at the Carnegie Library, a paragraph synopsis is created—indicated as an abstract—and a list of keywords/topics related to the content. The transcriber and the person who reviews the transcript both are encouraged to help with the abstract and word list, and the program coordinator monitors and contributes to descriptions. Dating back to 2010 and 2011, the library started thinking critically about metadata at a time when the national Oral History Association began enlisting members in conversation (see *Oral History Core: An Idea for a Metadata Scheme*[3]). To be blunt: The library's capture of metadata has been a fluid and evolving exercise, as time and hindsight have updated and informed what is thought to be "best." Chapter Three addressed metadata in great detail *because* this area is freshly showing to be one that hasn't received enough attention.

Working with Catalogs/Information Retrieval Systems

Bib Records and Items

With resources that are one of a kind, cataloging can turn inventive, and that's certainly been the case with Carnegie's oral histories, as perspectives and opinions have changed. But the real challenge to consistency is due to the longevity of the oral history program, which has been around long enough to see cassette tapes, VHS tapes, mini DV tapes, CDs, DVDs, WAV files, MP3s, and so on. For a *single* interview, the library might have two cassette tapes, a CD, two MP3 files, a transcript, a summary, and a file folder with a family genealogy. How do you show all of *that* in a bibliographic record? Ah, but remember: At the time when the bib record was created (let's say 1978), the two cassette tapes—sitting on a shelf—were the only evidence of the oral history. Those were the good old days.

Imagine you are using an online catalog, you type a keyword search for "oral history tennis," and you get three results—one of which shows with a call number of "OH0784 Audio Tape." ("Audio tape" is in the call number.) Probably you would conclude that the interview is available only as a cassette. This is problematic, because at some point the interview is likely to be digitized and, perhaps, made available online. Formats are sure to change, and the options for delivering formats will change; the one aspect that endures is the firsthand experience as told in the oral history. Thoughtful description of the oral history *content* is the priority.

Still, the catalog's job is to hold surrogate information that accurately reflects what can be experienced by the public. Working with a MARC record, the

> Thoughtful description of the oral history *content* is the priority.

700 fields can be used to add details about new manifestations if and when they emerge—a transcript, CD, flash drive, or whatever. Those details should not go into a fixed field, such as title or call number. One decision that has endured with Carnegie oral histories is item-level description versus collection level (archival materials often are grouped as collections). Even when interviews are part of a series and stem from the same source, each interview receives its own treatment in the catalog, its own description, and its own record. This has been the most profitable decision, in terms of connecting audience with oral history.

Beyond Catalogs

Of course, many libraries are stepping away from the MARC format altogether. The Carnegie Library is embarking on a wholesale shift, to provide better access to the library's entire collection of digital resources, with a new web platform forthcoming. The schema used on the new platform is Metadata Object Description Schema (MODS); however, the more critical shift is one of *thinking*.

For oral history, the opportunities are exciting. Within the entire collection of voices, defined sets of topical interviews can be used to explore the Semantic Web, publishing metadata using the Resource Description Framework. Word documents once were used to place information into a MARC record and into the BPL catalog; now those docs can be used to supplement the traditional catalog and publish directly to the web (once the learning curve is surmounted). After all, the World Wide Web is a massive, ingenious system for information retrieval. Moving beyond the limitations of traditional cataloging, the message of oral history will be better positioned for discovery.

DISSEMINATION: REACH

More frustrating than not knowing of an interview's existence is the instance of being well aware of an oral history, wanting to explore the interview, and finding no means of receiving the content. MROHP has a few oral histories that have been embargoed—meaning, the narrator has requested that public access be denied until a particular date, such as a year when the narrator predictably would have died. That situation forces the library to place a "tickler" on the interview—and then, on the specified date, reverse whatever has been done to keep the oral history out of public reach. Occasionally, a narrator requests that an interview be available only to those who come to the library—a soft barrier to access. The majority of the time, thankfully, narrators want their interviews to see the light of day and be received by the public. People who agree to be interviewed understand the importance of what they are creating for the community and feel gratified by the library's commitment to providing access.

Delivering Content

MROHP always has emphasized the recording of the interview as the primary source, versus transcript or other manifestation. Preceding the now-common awareness for digitization as a reformatting necessity, the program saw the need for having analog recordings converted to MP3 files. This allowed a pioneering foray into online streaming of audio, via a website built for the oral history program and tweaked between 2003 and 2005. The connection to voice was established, and, too, the library pictured an audience for the interviews beyond just the Boulder community. That first website had an untimely demise in 2013, when the platform on which it was created suffered breaches, and a variety of factors prohibited ongoing support and maintenance. Online access was cut off for eight months while plan B was formulated. So, a cautionary tale: Being on the cutting edge can draw blood.

Virtual Portals

In planning an online delivery system, think about long-term stability, continuity, and the likelihood of support. BPL was lucky that a hire had the experience to help parse out the pros and cons of different options. The correct fit turned out to be a WordPress site, locally hosted and tailored for the needs of oral history: a play function for audio, a tab for descriptive information (abstract, keywords/tags, names, and topics), a tab for transcript display, and a tab for display of photos. Searching for content is extremely easy and obvious—from the home page, a large box says SEARCH THE ORAL HISTORIES and advises to try "name, topic, or keyword." People also have the option to browse by special collections or browse by an alphabetical display using narrators' last names.

On the downside, no advance search is configured, and the match logic—which searches all descriptive data—is loose. For example, Boulder has a historic neighborhood called Martin Acres. A search for "Martin Acres" pulls up 59 results, including entries where only the word "Martin" appears, only the word "acres" appears, or the word "Martinez" appears. That said, the

display shows "most relevant" results first, so probably the first 40 returns
are about Martin Acres.

The website allows the download of transcripts in PDF format, but no
audio download. A main objective is to provide everything a researcher, family member, or casual browser would need to experience the interviews virtu-
ally—and the effort has been effective. Google Analytics calculates the
number of times people arrive at that site, in addition to online "visits" with
discrete interviews, which has been in the range of 20,000 to 25,000 per year
(this includes library staff). Sometimes, of course, the Internet does not
deliver everything needed.

Physical/Tactile Portals

With the WordPress site so successful, rarely do individuals come to the
library specifically to access the oral histories. More often, individuals are
exploring other onsite materials and then discover interviews, which they
may listen to on premises. Still, you will encounter long-distance situations
that demand a personal exchange.

The library was contacted by an individual living in the Czech Republic
who had studied psychology at the University of Colorado in the late
1960s. This man was interested in an interview with a professor who had
been his tutor; he was preparing a course about the professor, to be used in
the School of Social Studies at Masaryk University in Brno. MROHP was
delighted to share a direct link to the online interview, which included a full
transcript. The man was grateful—but he hoped to receive a copy of the
recording, to excerpt portions that he could play during a lecture. This precisely is the reason to have CDs or DVDs (or flash drives) ready for burning
files. With a signed statement attesting that the interview will be used for education, the library is happy to provide physical copies at minimal cost.
In return, the gentleman suggested that he'd like to donate copies of photos
taken in Boulder in the late 1960s—these can be part of a folder housed at
the library or rendered digitally for online display. The library does keep a
physical folder for each and every narrator, into which a transcript is placed,
and where complementary documents or photos might be placed.

Building Bridges to the Community

Explanation and Promotion

Effective oral history messaging is passionate and explicit. Occasionally, a
person will be identified as a strong candidate for interview but be wary or
unsure—wanting to know more about the experience and the anticipated
outcomes. This opportunity for initial conversation is exciting; this is when
a spark can be shared, when results can be shown. The outcome for the narrator might be captured, literally, during the oral history recording, when the

interview is winding down and the narrator says something like: "At first I didn't know what to expect, but you did a great job of explaining the process, and I thoroughly enjoyed myself." Success!

The follow-up comes when the recording is gifted back to the narrator. MROHP now offers either a physical copy on optical media (CD or DVD) or an electronic version that can be downloaded, copied, shared, and stored for posterity. Whatever choice is made by the narrator, a letter of Thank You reinforces previous messages of gratitude and explains the means by which the interview is publicly accessible.

Interview participants are the unofficial emissaries of the program, but other promotional outlets get utilized as well. The BPL website includes information about oral history, as does a bimonthly Events and Programs booklet and the library's annual report. At different times, the local newspaper has pushed promos about oral history, when special collections are newly established or when interview excerpts are looped and available for playback at the library. Also, on one occasion, the program coordinator was interviewed on a local radio station, speaking about oral history in general, the program specifically, and some of the more inspirational aspects of conducting interviews for a public library.

Programming and Presentations

Outreach work is most readily and successfully developed around special collections that give perspective to complex topics. For BPL, one of the most high-yielding sets of interviews has been a collection focusing on the Rocky Flats nuclear weapons plant, which produced bomb components between 1953 and 1992. The history of that facility—now entirely dismantled and described as "cleaned up"—included myriad angles for consideration: government officials, workers, scientists, activists, protestors, environmentalists, and regulators, to name some. With so many lenses for exploring the topic of the weapons plant, equally abundant are the options for engaging those viewpoints, using different formats. Interviews have been the basis for print materials, documentaries, a website, a community forum, and a forthcoming art exhibit.

When you develop a quantity of interviews, and you shed light on interesting people or topics, expect to be recognized for that accomplishment and asked to give talks. The program coordinator for MROHP

> The voices of the collection always, and most effectively, deliver a presentation's takeaway message.

has presented to a senior citizens' group, a religious group, a college class, a library department, a special-library association, and a meeting with city officials. Participation in local and national conferences also is a strong possibility; presentations involving oral history have a "wow" factor—interview clips enliven humdrum talking points and tug on the emotions of the audience. The voices of the collection always, and most effectively, deliver a presentation's takeaway message.

FINALLY: REWARDS

Hardly seems possible that you could have come this far without observing the benefits of bringing oral history into your library. Still, in the interest of being thorough, more selling points are forthcoming—including ideas about how to draw funding and stretch dollars. But dollars aren't the starting point. The starting point is people. You will find your greatest reward in relationships, contacts, and the response you receive from community. What you hear back—the words spoken about the library—will be the extra jingle in your pocket.

> *I am so appreciative of your efforts. This [restored audio file] will make a beautiful surprise for both my mother and her twin sister. . . . Please extend my sincere thanks to everyone on your team that made this possible.* (Community Member)

Unpaid Staff Are Library Champions

Another word for "unpaid staff" or "library champion" is volunteer. When asked about why they are motivated to volunteer for a library, most people offer that they have appreciated years of library services and want to *give back*. They are library champions. Another word for volunteer—okay, two words—is foot soldier. Foot soldiers carry out the important and sometimes difficult work of an organization; they are boots on the ground, getting things done. For an oral history program, nothing is more important than volunteers who are invested in the idea of community knowledge and local history. A coordinator's job is to organize a system for harnessing that energy, enthusiasm, and commitment, ensuring that outcomes are in line with the library's overall mission.

Demonstrated in the preceding chapters—and in this chapter—is the fact that oral history involves myriad tasks in order to bring interviews into existence and then make them accessible. MROHP provides a menu of opportunities for volunteers, allowing individuals to select areas where their personality, interest, and time are best exercised. The program is broken into discrete tasks—not unlike a production line—and this arrangement draws people who want to take responsibility for defined/limited sets of work. Some volunteers are retired professionals who have skills that might not have been showcased as part of their job life but can be featured as part of MROHP. But volunteers' ages range widely—youth in their twenties as well as octogenarians. (One of the program's sharpest interviewers dubbed himself Agent 096, which is 007 + his age of 89.) Here are specific comments offered by our volunteers, gathered and used for a presentation and, in the fall of 2008, an Oral History Association newsletter article:

- I find myself truly enjoying transcription: the attention to voice, cadence, and inflection is wholly absorbing.
- The structure of the program—the clear guidelines with respect to doing the oral histories, getting releases, how to handle equipment, how to do transcripts—and the training provided has been tremendously important to me.
- Having the responsibility for actually delivering is unusual in many volunteer jobs.
- I love the experience of capturing for posterity individual personal histories that contribute unique bits or pieces to the larger "public" history.[4]

Largely because of its oral history program, BPL was nominated for the 2018 National Medal for Museum and Library Service, which recognizes contributions to the community and "honors institutions that demonstrate extraordinary approaches to serving their constituents and that exceed expected levels of community outreach." The oral history program specifically was cited by the individual who made the nomination, one of Colorado's senators. Being acknowledged and called out for attention was a tremendous honor. But more gratifying was the letter of support written by one of MROHP's long-standing volunteers, parts of which are repeated here:

I have been a volunteer with the Maria Rogers Oral History Program for more than 15 years. I was attracted to the program partly because it is integrated into the local history branch of the public library, which made it to my mind a community-based program. ...

Since the mission of the oral history collection is to record the perspectives and experiences of ordinary people as well as those with special expertise or leadership, the trove of oral histories includes interviews that have helped build a fuller, deeper history of our community. ...

I have come to understand that the oral history program is especially valued by those who are interviewed (and their families). They are grateful that their particular contributions are understood, valued, and retained for posterity. ...

I realize that as a volunteer dedicated to this program, I may be biased. Nevertheless, I feel I understand the program's contribution to the community over a significant period of time. Because the program is primarily "staffed" by volunteers, the resources needed to keep the program functioning are modest. I truly believe it is a treasure for the community, as well as an asset for the Boulder Public Library.

The letter is beautifully written and magnificently detailed. The words are an overwhelming gift to the library and to the oral history program.

Relation Building and Cross Promotion

Over the decades, MROHP has benefitted from many fruitful collaborations that have led to new oral histories and/or exposure to the library's existing body of voices. In 2016, the City of Boulder approached the library to ask for help in planning a public-education series about the history of the Community Hospital, which was under review for potential reuse. During initial meetings, ideas were exchanged about how to gather new recollections and/or how to utilize existing materials. The decision was to cull from existing photos as well as existing oral histories to create a mini documentary about the hospital—to explain changes to the brick-and-mortar structures and changes in land use and to document peoples' experiences with the hospital over the duration of its life span. The result was a 20-minute video (photos paired with audio) that played in a "community engagement" room associated with the hospital's redevelopment plans. The video itself worked as an advertisement for MROHP—as did surrounding signage and all of the city's promotional material.

Funding and In-Kind Support

Let me refer back to the two previous sections on relation building and library champions—because those two ingredients are most likely to bring actual dollars to an oral history project/program, in addition to the underlying equitable exchange. You do not undertake oral history to make money, but the possibility exists for getting funds that allow work above and beyond what you ordinarily would accomplish—or to pay for something specific like a website redesign. A simple way to start growing a reserve is to ask for donations from community members. This doesn't need to be an awkward pitch. Include a donation form along with the gift CD (or flash drive) that gets mailed to narrators. Or send a letter when the oral history has been fully processed and is available through the library catalog—and include a donation form with that letter. Oral history generates tremendous good will and appreciation; catalyze on that sentiment and make a simple "ask." Even nominal donations of $10 or $20 add up—and, equally important, the existence of small donations can leverage bigger sums from granting agencies or philanthropists who want proof of community support.

If you are determined to pursue a grant, be aware that the process can be extremely tedious and time consuming, and the ratio of applications to award recipients is not encouraging. So think about grant money *only* for projects/ideas that are gravy and not necessity. An example that is not theoretical: When I was an intern with the Maria Rogers Program, I learned how to do everything involved with processing an interview (transcribing, describing, cataloging, loading to the website, etc.). The coordinator at the time encouraged me to pursue funding to pay myself to process a collection of interviews that had been offered to the library. The interviews had been conducted by an independent researcher and would complement the existing body of oral histories documenting the Rocky Flats weapons plant, but the library was hesitant to take the donation, because so many other oral histories already were in the pipeline, and the new interviews were on cassettes so first would need to be digitized.

Long story short: I did pursue funding and received a nice sum from Colorado Humanities. The learning process was invaluable, and the library itself did not bear the brunt of time expenditure—the majority was on me as an intern. So, not the worst idea from the perspective of the library: Offer to volunteers that if they want to shoulder the responsibility for seeking funding, a project is available.

The subject of grant proposals is deep and complicated and is the fodder for countless books, courses, and web resources. Also, grants are not necessarily the most sensible first choice for funding regular oral history work—grants are best for specific, well-defined projects that might otherwise go unexplored. Think instead about dollars in the surrounding community: Who are your local philanthropists or business people? What are their social concerns? Do you have existing content—or ideas for interviews—that relate to those concerns? Can you demonstrate that you have a process for getting things done? Predictability is your ally and will encourage individuals or organizations to support your work, because the return on investment is solid.

Thank you so much for all the work you and your staff have done. . . . These oral histories will be of benefit for many generations to come. (Community Member)

FINAL FINISHING THOUGHTS

I wish that I had saved a jaw-dropping nugget of wisdom that would poetically, poignantly, and perfectly conclude the message of this book. Unfortunately, all was spent in the preceding pages, and I fear that if you haven't received the spirit by now, you likely will remain untouched. Still, one small item may have been forgotten—a haiku that appeared almost at the beginning:

> *reality is*
> *imagination that has*
> *become consensus*

When you imagine something, you see it; when you see it, you believe it; when you believe it, it's real. I hope this book has given you a picture that is real enough to pursue. I hope that you have come to a consensus about the power and possibility of oral history, and you will make *oral history in your library* a reality.

And lastly: The appendix to this book shows something imaginative that might just be coming. . . .

NOTES

1. The website for the Boulder County Latino History Project is http:// bocolatinohistory.colorado.edu/. Lead organizer for the project, Marjorie McIntosh, worked with MROHP throughout 2013 and 2014.

2. Mark Greene and Dennis Meissner, "More Product, Less Process: Revamping Traditional Archival Processing," *The American Archivist*, Fall/Winter 2005, vol. 68, no. 2, pp. 208–263.

3. Nancy MacKay, "Oral History Core: An Idea for a Metadata Scheme," in Oral History in the Digital Age, edited by Doug Boyd, Steve Cohen, Brad Rakerd, and Dean Rehberger (Washington, DC: Institute of Museum and Library Services, 2012). http://ohda.matrix.msu.edu/2012/06/oral-history-core/.

4. Susan Becker, "The Maria Rogers Oral History Program: Volunteers Plus Technology = Preservation and Access." *Oral History Association Newsletter*, Fall 2008, vol. XLII, no. 2, p. 5.

Appendix

Colorado Voice Preserve

Oʀᴀʟ Hɪsᴛᴏʀʏ is the process of recording and preserving memories that reflect firsthand experiences. *"Oral sources tell us not just what people did, but what they wanted to do, what they believed they were doing, and what they now think they did"* (historian and author Alessandro Portelli).

Oᴘᴘᴏʀᴛᴜɴɪᴛʏ

Oral history projects can target individuals and social groups who have been marginalized; firsthand stories can challenge a "status quo" understanding or a controlled message. **In March 2012, a Colorado assessment showed that 96% of the state's oral histories are not fully accessible.** An infrastructure dedicated to oral history would put 100% of its resources toward making 100% of interviews discoverable, available, understandable, and usable.

Pᴜʀᴘᴏsᴇ

Colorado Voice Preserve (CVP) will work with libraries, museums, and community groups to develop oral history content: identifying projects, loaning equipment, and supplying interview guidelines/protocols that ensure placement in the digital repository. Trained volunteers will assist with interview processing: transcribing audio; creating abstracts, keyword listings, and subject headings; prepping interviews for online search utilities; and posting interviews for web dissemination. The mission is to connect our public with stories that explain the human consequence of events and decisions.

Impact

Oral history is not itself an end. The recorded interview is raw material for new expressions of understanding: books, presentations, exhibits, and documentaries. But that raw potential can't be harnessed unless voices are preserved and made accessible. CVP embraces that responsibility, bringing oral histories into useful life so the captured voice fulfills its prophecy of informing public thought and action.

Multidisciplinary Collaboration

CVP is supported by History Colorado, Colorado Humanities, and the Colorado State Library.

- The functional purpose of **History Colorado** is to collect, preserve, and interpret the state's history for present and future generations. The larger ambition is to engage citizens in Colorado's tradition and legacy.
- The humanities provide tools for examining the human experience and asking fundamental questions of purpose and meaning. **Colorado Humanities** brings these tools to communities via literary, cultural, and historical programs.
- The **Colorado State Library** provides leadership and expertise in developing library-related standards, activities, and services for school, public, academic, and special libraries.

References

Boyd, Doug. 2014. "I Just Want to Click on It to Listen: Oral History Archives, Orality, and Usability." In *Oral History and Digital Humanities: Voice, Access, and Engagement*, edited by Mary Larson and Doug Boyd, 77–88. New York: Palgrave Macmillan.

Boyd, Doug and Mary Larson, ed. 2014. *Oral History and Digital Humanities: Voice, Access, and Engagement*. New York: Palgrave Macmillan.

Burkeman, Oliver. 2002. "Voice of America." *The Guardian* (February 28). https://www.theguardian.com/books/2002/mar/01/studsterkel.

Hendrigan, Holly. 2017. "Naturals with a Microphone: Oral History and the Librarian Skillset." In *ACRL 2017 Proceedings*. Baltimore, MD, March 22–25.

Lankes, R. David. 2011. *The Atlas of New Librarianship*. Cambridge, MA: The MIT Press.

Pearce-Moses, Richard. 2005. *A Glossary of Archival and Records Terminology*. Chicago: Society of American Archivists.

Ritchie, Donald A. 2003. *Doing Oral History: A Practical Guide*, Second Edition. New York: Oxford University Press, Inc.

Zachert, Martha Jane K. 1968. "The Implications of Oral History for Librarians," *College & Research Libraries* 29, no. 2 (March): 101–103.

Index

About the Author and Contributor

CYNTHIA "CYNS" NELSON coordinates the Maria Rogers Oral History Program at the Carnegie Library for Local History in Boulder, Colorado. Cyns is a professional librarian with experience leading, consulting on, and contributing to oral history projects throughout Colorado. She has been a guest lecturer for San Jose State University and has taught regional and national oral history workshops, including for the Veterans History Project of the Library of Congress. Passion for libraries and oral history fuels her aspirations; poetry has been a creative force.

ADAM SPEIRS managed the oral history collection for the Douglas County History Research Center at Douglas County Libraries in Colorado from 2012 to 2017. He has worked in academic, private, public library, and government archives since 2007 and currently works with Denver Water, Colorado's oldest and largest water utility. He has presented at state and national conferences on the intersection of oral history and public libraries and on other topics.